Wild Goose Marina, Inc.

Microsoft® Windows® Version CD-ROM

A Computerized Business Simulation

Third Edition

Leland Mansuetti
Sierra College

Keith Weidkamp
Sierra College

Irwin McGraw-Hill

Boston   Burr Ridge, IL   Dubuque, IA   Madison, WI   New York   San Francisco   St. Louis
Bangkok   Bogotá   Caracas   Lisbon   London   Madrid
Mexico City   Milan   New Delhi   Seoul   Singapore   Sydney   Taipei   Toronto

McGraw-Hill Higher Education

A Division of The McGraw-Hill Companies

WILD GOOSE MARINA, INC., MICROSOFT® WINDOWS® VERSION CD-ROM, A COMPUTERIZED
BUSINESS SIMULATION
Leland Mansuetti and Keith Weidkamp

Published by Irwin/McGraw-Hill, an imprint of the McGraw-Hill Companies, Inc., 1221 Avenue of the
Americas, New York, NY 10020. Copyright © 2000, 1996, 1993 by the McGraw-Hill Companies, Inc. All
rights reserved.

2 3 4 5 6 7 8 9 0 BKM/BKM 0 9 8 7 6 5 4 3 2

ISBN 0-07-234620-5

www.mhhe.com

DEDICATED TO OUR FAMILIES

Janet

Linda, Aaron, Kristin, Zachary

ACKNOWLEDGMENTS

The Accounting Students of Sierra College
Rocklin, California

Mellisa Davis and Cara Furbee

PREFACE

The **Wild Goose Marina, Incorporated**, computerized practice set has been designed with two important objectives in mind. First and foremost, the student will receive a thorough review of all the major accounting concepts found in <u>Financial Accounting</u> and in the introduction to <u>Intermediate Accounting</u>. While reviewing these concepts, the student will become familiar with a computerized accounting system similar to commercial systems found in the business world. The computer will quickly and efficiently take care of all of the time consuming bookkeeping tasks and statement preparation and give the student time for statement evaluation and decision making.

Sophisticated, yet easy to use, software will allow the student to work very rapidly and efficiently through a variety of business transactions. At the end of each accounting session (7-8 days and 22-30 transactions) the student will find a convenient **"Check It Out"** block to compare account balances and trial balance totals. If errors are found, the student will simply follow the audit trail provided, locate the errors, and then make the necessary corrections. **Mid-project** (June 15) and **final-project evaluations** (June 30, the end of the second quarter) will be performed by printing selected documents and answering a series of analytical questions. This process will provide a detailed review of the financial information. Time originally spent preparing the documents will now be spent evaluating the statements and the business operations.

The **Wild Goose Marina, Incorporated,** accounting system is designed in a Windows format. Data entry is accomplished using a general journal screen for journalizing and validation. After entering the date, the chart of accounts is accessed with a mouse click. The chart may be used directly for data entry or each account may be entered manually. A calculator is available for immediate calculation of amounts to be entered and the calculated total may be "pasted" directly into a debit or credit column. The amount of the credit entry can be automatically entered using the **C Key**. Printing documents for review and analysis is quick and easy. The general journal (all or part), general ledger, accounts receivable and accounts payable ledgers can be brought to the screen for quick review and/or printing. These printed documents, as well as the multiple-step financial statements, provide the information for a detailed analysis of the business operations.

Special features of the business simulation include an **automatic closing** option which allows the student to close the books quickly and efficiently with a single keystroke. The closing entry procedure, which is so time consuming when completed manually, is similar to many commercial systems. A **reinstatement option** allows the student to reopen the accounts, if necessary, for error correction purposes. This allows better use of time for important analysis and evaluation of the Wild Goose Marina, Incorporated, operations. A new **Reset** option allows the student to reset the disk back to the June 1 beginning balances any time <u>prior to the start of the second week of transactions</u>.

The overall objective of this practice set is to provide students an opportunity to use, review, and learn a very significant amount of financial/corporate accounting information in a very short period of time. Using this computerized accounting system allows the students to fully realize this objective, maximize their study time, and to move closer to the real world accounting and finance environment.

Leland Mansuetti

Keith Weidkamp

T A B L E   O F   C O N T E N T S

INTRODUCTION TO

WILD GOOSE MARINA, INCORPORATED

Wild Goose Marina, Incorporated, is a small corporation with offices and business facilities located at Gold Rush Reservoir in Northern California. The business operates on a long-term lease agreement to provide houseboat sales, service, and moorage for customers. Sales include both new and used houseboats. Service includes work on boats in the water and in dry dock. The company has special trailer and truck equipment to pull the largest houseboats from the lake for periodic pontoon, structure, and motor service. The company also installs, maintains, and rents moorage buoys for 175 houseboats. As an added feature for moorage customers, Wild Goose Marina provides ferry service, pump-out facilities, and 24-hour security. The gas and grocery sales, as well as the houseboat and personal watercraft rentals, are handled by another company and the two businesses share some of the launch ramp and security costs. Wild Goose Marina maintains first-class facilities and has become one of the top recreational areas in Northern California. New houseboat sales are steady and resales of used houseboats frequent. The service portion of the business has not been as strong as expected but has shown signs of growth as the company has increased equipment, facilities, and staff. Moorage rental has been 100% since the first year of operation and several customers are on a waiting list to acquire a moorage buoy. The company recently installed 50 additional buoys to help meet the demand.

To complete the on-the-job training requirement for your accounting course, you have been placed in a one-month internship program with Wild Goose Marina, Inc. You will be responsible for all of the accounting work from June 1 through June 30, including recording the accounting transactions, auditing your work, and correcting all errors. You will be responsible for the preparation and/or printing of several documents as you work through this accounting period. On June 15 and at the end of the month you will be required to print/prepare several documents for evaluation. Your responsibility on June 30 will include recording the adjusting entries, printing the financial statements, closing the books, and preparation of a thorough analysis of the business operations. The analysis will include a required final session using the computer generated financial documents to answer a series of questions. Optional problems may be completed as directed by your instructor. These may include an analysis of cash flows listing all investing and financing activities that were inflows and outflows of cash, a bond sinking fund schedule, and an alternative depreciation schedule for the fork lift. Since Wild Goose Marina, Inc., uses a computerized accounting system, this opportunity to obtain hands-on experience and practice your accounting skills should be very rewarding, as well as time-efficient.

The first step in operating the computerized system correctly is to review the chart of accounts. A **clear understanding** of how certain accounts are used by Wild Goose Marina, Inc., **is required before you begin the recording process**. A detailed explanation of how several accounts are used in the Wild Goose accounting system follows on the next five pages. Pages 7-10 list the full Chart of Accounts. Page 11 displays the customer list and vendor list with the account numbers used to identify these individuals and businesses when entering accounts receivable or accounts payable transactions. **Pages 12** and **13** summarize key business items to remember as you begin your accounting work. These pages also list the special keys and buttons that can be used to simplify the data entry process.

CHART OF ACCOUNTS

To properly enter the accounting transactions for Wild Goose Marina, Inc., you will need to familiarize yourself with the chart of accounts. The business has five revenue accounts. Four of the revenue accounts, **Houseboat Sales, Accessories & Parts Sales, Service Fees Earned,** and **Moorage Fees Earned**, are used to record transactions involving the sales and the services performed. For this set, sales tax (7%) is charged on **all merchandise and service sales.** Sales tax is not charged on Moorage Fees Earned. Fees received in advance for moorage fees are credited directly to the liability account, **Unearned Moorage Fees. Moorage Fees Earned** is adjusted at the end of each accounting period for all moorage fees **that have been earned. Sales Commissions Earned** is the fifth revenue account and is credited for the commissions earned in selling used houseboats for moorage customers.

Wild Goose Marina accepts **bank** credit cards for all customer charges except Houseboat Sales. When a customer purchases merchandise using a bank credit card, the sale is entered as a **cash sale.** The credit card expense is **not** recorded at the time of the sale. For bank card charges, the business is charged a credit card fee (**1-4%**) which is recorded from a bank statement received at the end of the month. Company credit cards are not accepted by Wild Goose Marina.

Several accounts which require special attention are listed below:

103 **Short Term Investments** is the current asset control account representing the total of short-term, marketable securities held by Wild Goose Marina.

105 **Accounts Receivable** is the control account for all customer accounts. Wild Goose Marina extends 30-day credit to all charge customers.

106 **Allowance for Doubtful Accounts** is the contra current asset account that is debited when bad debts are written off as uncollectible.

109 **Notes Receivable** is the control account for all short-term notes related to houseboat sales and past-due receivables.

113 **Interest Receivable** is normally used only for adjusting entries.

123 **Prepaid Insurance** is debited for the purchase of all insurance policies.

124 **Prepaid Rent** is debited for rent payments made for more than one month in advance. Wild Goose Marina has a long-term rental agreement and prepays rent for six months.

125 **Prepaid Property Tax** accounts for all property taxes paid in advance.

127 **Prepaid Advertising** is used only for adjusting entries. All advertising costs are debited directly to the Advertising Expense account.

129 **Office Supplies** is debited for all purchases of business supplies used in the office.

140 **Investment in Baldwin Manufacturing** accounts for a major, 30% investment in this manufacturing company. This is a long-term investment and Wild Goose Marina has a significant influence in the operations of this company.

141 **Long-Term Investments** accounts for investments made on a long-term basis that do not involve influential ownership or control of any firm whose stock is held. This account also lists the value of a parcel of land held for future development by Wild Goose Marina.

160 **Leasehold** has been debited for a long-term sub-lease. A portion of this leasehold is amortized to **Rent Expense** with an adjusting entry.

165 **Leasehold Improvements** to the rented/leased facilities have been made as needed to the mooring areas and to the launching ramp. A portion of these costs are amortized to the Rent Expense account with an adjusting entry.

170 **Patents** have been secured on a special houseboat trailer developed and now used by Wild Goose Marina. A portion of this cost is amortized at the end of each quarter.

211 **Sales Tax Payable** is the liability account used to account for all sales tax collections. For this practice set, **sales tax, at a rate of 7%, will be charged on all Houseboat Sales, Accessories & Parts Sales, and Service Fees Earned. Sales Tax will not be charged on Moorage Fees. Commissions earned on selling used houseboats for moorage customers will not involve sales tax collections. Excise or luxury taxes will not be a part of any of the transactions of this business simulation.**

215 **Unearned Moorage Fees** is credited for all moorage fees received in advance. Wild Goose Marina receives cash moorage payments from customers on a six-month or annual basis. The earned portion of these receipts are accounted for in the adjusting entry process at the end of each quarter.

235 **Long-Term Lease Liability** accounts for the liability assumed when a capital lease or financing lease for new shop equipment or other assets is signed.

236 **Discount on Lease Financing** is the contra liability account used with the Long-Term Lease Liability account in calculating the carrying value of the capital lease for shop equipment or other assets. The balance of this account is amortized to Interest Expense over the life of the lease.

241 **Long-Term Notes Payable** accounts for the liability assumed when a long-term, non-interest-bearing note is given for the acquisition of assets.

242 **Discount on Long-Term Notes Payable** is the contra liability account used with the Long-Term Notes Payable account in calculating the carrying value of the note. The total of this account is amortized to Interest Expense over the life of the note.

320 **Cash Dividends Declared** is debited for all cash dividend declarations. At the end of each accounting period the account is closed into Retained Earnings.

330 **Treasury Stock** accounts for all stock purchased back from stockholders **but not retired**. The stock can later be resold with the gains or losses on the transaction properly accounted for in the Contributed Capital--Treasury Stock Transactions or Retained Earnings account.

401 **Houseboat Sales** is a major revenue account of Wild Goose Marina, Inc. All houseboats sold for cash or on credit are credited to this account at the time of sale.

407 **Accessories & Parts Sales** accounts for the sale of all houseboat and marine accessories and parts. These sales may be cash sales, credit sales, or bank card sales.

408 **Accessories & Parts Sales Returns & Allowances** is debited for all returned merchandise. Credit memos are issued for all returned items.

412 **Service Fees Earned** accounts for the revenues earned by the performance of service work on customer houseboats. This includes regular maintenance, haulouts, pontoon stripping and sealing, lake-to-drydock hauling, and complete rebuilding. Adjustments in service charges (error correction) for a customer are debited directly to this account and a credit memo is issued. Service work is usually billed at **$60.00 per hour**.

415 **Moorage Fees Earned** is credited in the adjusting entry process at the end of each quarter for the total dollars earned for mooring and securing customer houseboats. Moorage fees are received for a minimum of 6-months from moorage customers and are credited initially to the Unearned Moorage Fees account.

420 **Sales Commissions Earned** accounts for all of the sales commissions earned for selling customer houseboats. A standard fee of 8% on the first $20,000 of the selling price and 2% on the balance over $20,000 is charged. The commission is collected at the time of the sale.

501 **Purchases--Houseboats** is the cost account debited for the purchase price of the houseboats.

502 **Purchases Discounts--Houseboats** accounts for the cash saved by taking advantage of the cash discounts extended by vendors.

503 **Transportation-In--Houseboats** is the cost account debited for all freight and hauling costs incurred in transporting houseboats to the Wild Goose Marina launching ramp.

506 **Purchases Returns & Allowances--Accessories & Parts** is credited for the value of all merchandise items returned to vendors. A debit memo is issued with all returns.

603 **Rent Expense** is adjusted at the end of each accounting period for an amortized portion of the Leasehold account. Leasehold improvements are amortized to the Rent Expense account. A portion of the Prepaid Rent is also charged to this account.

604 **Equipment Rental Expense** is debited for the monthly rental charges of equipment and for the monthly rental fees charged under all *operating leases*.

605 **Office Supplies Expense** is used only for adjusting entries.

606 **Service & Shop Supplies Expense** is used only for adjusting entries.

608 **Advertising Expense** is debited directly for all advertising fees incurred.

609 **Credit Card Expense** accounts for bank credit card fees charged to Wild Goose Marina, Inc., for customer use of their bank credit cards. The credit card fees range between 1 and 4 percent of the total amount of the customer charge. The credit card expense will be accounted for with a single summary entry at the end of the month. Wild Goose Marina accepts bank cards in payment for accessories, parts, service, and moorage.

611 **Tools Expense** is debited for the purchase of all miscellaneous tools used in the shop and in servicing customer houseboats. The relatively small cost of these items does not warrant capitalizing and depreciating the assets.

621 **Payroll Tax Expense** accounts for the employer taxes including FICA taxes and State and Federal Unemployment taxes.

622 **Insurance Expense** is adjusted at the end of each accounting period.

623 **Bad Debt Expense** is estimated at the end of each accounting period in the adjusting entry procedure. Wild Goose Marina uses the aging method to estimate bad debts.

624 **Property Tax Expense** accounts for the property taxes for the period charged against the assets of the business.

627 **Bank Service Charges** is debited for all check printing costs and checking account fees.

629 **License Expense** is debited for the cost of all business and vehicle license fees.

630 **Professional Services Expense** is debited for the cost of all tax, accounting, and legal services received by the business.

713 **Dividends Earned** is an **Other Revenue** account that is credited for dividends earned on short-term investments.

721 **Gain on Sale of Assets** is an **Other Revenue** account that is credited when the proceeds from the sale of a Plant and Equipment asset are greater than the book value of the asset. This account is **not used** in like-kind exchange (trade) transactions.

731   **Gain On Short-Term Investments** is credited when the proceeds of an investment sale exceed the original basis of the investment.

821   **Loss on Sale/Disposal of Assets** is an **Other Expense** account that is debited when a Plant and Equipment asset is sold and the proceeds of the sale are less than the book value of the asset. This account is also used to account for the loss incurred when an asset with book value is donated or given away. On like-kind exchange (trade) transactions, this account is **not used**.

831   **Loss on Short-Term Investments** is debited when the proceeds from the sale of an investment are less than the original basis of the investment.

Entering Transactions And Using The Chart Of Accounts

Special data entry procedures that will make your work more efficient have been built into the new Wild Goose Marina accounting system. When entering transactions, all of the accounts will be identified by account number. You will see the account title appear instantly on the screen as you enter the account number. With the cursor at the account prompt the chart of accounts can be displayed on the screen with a click on the **Chart** command button.

Customer and Vendor Lists

Detailed information on customer and vendor account activity and balances will be maintained automatically in the Accounts Receivable and Accounts Payable ledgers. Information will be recorded in the system by identifying each customer or vendor/creditor by number. When the customer or vendor prompt appears, type the vendor or customer number or click on the list box and select the appropriate vendor or customer.

CHART OF ACCOUNTS
WILD GOOSE MARINA, INCORPORATED

ASSETS

101	Cash
102	Petty Cash
103	Short-Term Investments
105	Accounts Receivable
106	Allowance for Doubtful Accounts
109	Notes Receivable
113	Interest Receivable
115	Subscriptions Receivable--Preferred Stock
116	Subscriptions Receivable--Common Stock
117	Merchandise Inventory--Houseboats
119	Merchandise Inventory--Accessories & Parts
123	Prepaid Insurance
124	Prepaid Rent
125	Prepaid Property Tax
127	Prepaid Advertising
129	Office Supplies
131	Service & Shop Supplies
140	Investment in Baldwin Manufacturing
141	Long-Term Investments
142	Bond Sinking Fund
145	Service & Shop Equipment
146	Accumulated Depreciation, Service & Shop Equipment
149	Trucks
150	Accumulated Depreciation, Trucks
153	Trailers
154	Accumulated Depreciation, Trailers
157	Office Equipment
158	Accumulated Depreciation, Office Equipment
160	Leasehold
165	Leasehold Improvements
170	Patents
175	Organization Costs

LIABILITIES

201	Accounts Payable
202	Interest Payable
203	Short-Term Notes Payable
204	Discount on Short-Term Notes Payable
205	Legal Fees Payable

(liabilities continued on next page)

CHART OF ACCOUNTS
WILD GOOSE MARINA, INCORPORATED

(liabilities continued)

206	Preferred Cash Dividends Payable
208	Common Cash Dividends Payable
209	Salaries & Wages Payable
211	Sales Tax Payable
212	Estimated Property Taxes Payable
213	Income Taxes Payable
215	Unearned Moorage Fees
221	Employees' Federal Income Taxes Payable
223	FICA Taxes Payable
225	State Unemployment Taxes Payable
227	Federal Unemployment Taxes Payable
235	Long-Term Lease Liability
236	Discount on Lease Financing
241	Long-Term Notes Payable
242	Discount on Long-Term Notes Payable
250	Bonds Payable
251	Discount on Bonds Payable
252	Premium on Bonds Payable

STOCKHOLDERS' EQUITY

301	Preferred Stock
302	Preferred Stock Subscribed
303	Contributed Capital in Excess of Par, Preferred Stock
304	Contributed Capital--Retirement of Preferred Stock
305	Common Stock
306	Common Stock Subscribed
307	Common Stock Dividend Distributable
308	Contributed Capital in Excess of Par, Common Stock
309	Contributed Capital--Retirement of Common Stock
310	Contributed Capital--Treasury Stock Transactions
315	Retained Earnings
320	Cash Dividends Declared
325	Stock Dividends Declared
330	Treasury Stock

CHART OF ACCOUNTS
WILD GOOSE MARINA, INCORPORATED

REVENUE

401	Houseboat Sales
407	Accessories & Parts Sales
408	Accessories & Parts Sales Returns & Allowances
412	Service Fees Earned
415	Moorage Fees Earned
420	Sales Commissions Earned

COST OF GOODS SOLD

501	Purchases--Houseboats
502	Purchases Discounts--Houseboats
503	Transportation-In--Houseboats
505	Purchases--Accessories & Parts
506	Purchases Returns & Allowances--Accessories & Parts
507	Purchases Discounts--Accessories & Parts
508	Transportation-In--Accessories & Parts

OPERATING EXPENSES

601	Office & Shop Salaries & Wages Expense
602	Executive & Salesperson Salaries
603	Rent Expense
604	Equipment Rental Expense
605	Office Supplies Expense
606	Service & Shop Supplies Expense
607	Truck Operating Expense
608	Advertising Expense
609	Credit Card Expense
610	Delivery Expense
611	Tools Expense
613	Depreciation Expense, Service & Shop Equipment
615	Depreciation Expense, Trucks
617	Depreciation Expense, Trailers
619	Depreciation Expense, Office Equipment
621	Payroll Tax Expense
622	Insurance Expense
623	Bad Debt Expense
624	Property Tax Expense
625	Electric & Gas Expense

(expenses continued on next page)

CHART OF ACCOUNTS
WILD GOOSE MARINA, INCORPORATED

(expenses continued)

626   Telephone Expense
627   Bank Service Charges
628   Cash Short and Over
629   License Expense
630   Professional Services Expense
631   Janitorial Services Expense
632   Amortization Expense--Patents
633   Amortization Expense--Organization Costs
635   Miscellaneous Expense

OTHER REVENUE

711   Interest Earned
713   Dividends Earned
715   Earnings on Investment in Baldwin Manufacturing
721   Gain on Sale of Assets
725   Gain on Retirement of Bonds
731   Gain on Short-Term Investments
741   Miscellaneous Revenue

OTHER EXPENSE

811   Income Tax Expense
813   Interest Expense
821   Loss on Sale/Disposal of Assets
825   Loss on Retirement of Bonds
831   Loss on Short-Term Investments
835   Loss on Long-Term Investments

901   Income Summary

Wild Goose Marina, Incorporated
Customer List

Customer Number	Customer
10200	Adams Farms, Incorporated
10550	Bettencourt, Incorporated
10820	R. J. Corsetti
11050	J. P. Elam
11185	Joan Kuhlman
11260	Kingston & Sons, Incorporated
11350	Dale Novice
11405	Randy Robberts
11470	Roseburg & Associates
11520	Taylor Company
11695	Tisedaile Construction Co.
11920	Zakk, Incorporated

Wild Goose Marina, Incorporated
Vendor List

Vendor Number	Vendor
20500	Corr Marine Supply
21990	Foster Business Supply
22600	Kruzer Houseboats
24800	Luzzi, Incorporated
25950	Quinlivin, Incorporated
26675	Reading Real Estate
27005	Rockwood Business Supply
27125	Snow Goose Houseboats
28400	Yee & Associates, Incorporated

KEY DETAILS TO REMEMBER AS YOU JOURNALIZE TRANSACTIONS

To properly and efficiently operate the computerized accounting system used by Wild Goose Marina, Incorporated, you must be familiar with several important computer procedures as well as business and account information details. These procedures and details are summarized in the list below and are introduced and explained in detail in the data entry procedures of the first week of your internship (June 1-8).

The **Chart** button may be used at **any account prompt** to display the **Chart of Accounts**. The chart of accounts may be used for faster data entry as well as for a quick reference to the number of each account in the chart of accounts.

After the debit entry or entries have been recorded, **Pressing the C key** will automatically enter the amount of the credit entry (last credit entry if more than one credit).

A customer list with customer account numbers will be available when the Accounts Receivable account is a part of the journal entry.

All charge customers are extended 30-day credit by Wild Goose Marina. Customer balances that are over thirty days are considered past-due balances.

A vendor list with the vendor (creditor) account numbers will be available when the Accounts Payable account is a part of the journal entry.

When entering transactions, always use proper accounting procedure and enter the debit entries **first**. When **debits** equal **credits** you will have a complete transaction to verify.

When several entries are to be entered on the <u>same day</u>, after the first journal entry has been entered and verified, click on the **Repeat Date** button to automatically enter the date for each subsequent transaction.

Error correction procedures for the Wild Goose system require that the incorrect entry **be backed out (reversed)** and **then reentered correctly**. This correction procedure will be introduced in the first few transactions of the project. When an invoice number prompt, item prompt, or overhead prompt appears when entering a back out entry, enter **ERROR**. If an **error correction entry for cash** requires a credit to cash (and a check is not being issued), enter **ERROR** at the check number prompt. Additional detailed error correction instructions will be presented at the first check point (the end of the first week of transactions).

You may terminate a journalizing session **at any time**. When you return to the journal entry process at a later time, the last entry recorded will be displayed on the screen.

At the end of each week, audit your work and make all of the necessary corrections required to match the "Check It Out" box. If printed documents are required, you must print the items **before continuing to the next week of transactions**. The system does not store end-of-week balances that can be printed later.

When computing **sales tax, credit card fees, interest,** or **purchase discounts** always round the final amount **to the nearest cent**.

Sales tax of **7%** is charged on all sales and labor. Sales tax is **not charged** on Moorage Fees. No excise or luxury taxes are used in this business simulation. Be sure to round to the nearest cent when necessary.

Labor charges will be billed to customers at a rate of **$60.00 per hour**.

A May 31, 2001 Trial Balance, Schedule of Accounts Receivable, and **Schedule of Accounts Payable** are shown in the Appendix.

WILD GOOSE MARINA, INCORPORATED

INSTALLING THE PROGRAM

AND BEGINNING

THE TRANSACTIONS

INSTALLING THE PROGRAM

Installation Using the CD-ROM

1. **Close all applications that may be running (such as MS WinWord or MS Excell).**
2. Insert the **CD-ROM disk** in the appropriate drive.
3. Click on **Start,** then click on **Run**.
4. Type the letter of the disk drive, followed by :\Setup   Example: **D:\Setup**
5. Press the **Enter key**.
6. At the first prompt, click on **OK** if all applications have been closed.
7. At the next prompt, **click** on the button with the **monitor icon** to install the program on the default drive and folder, **C:\Program Files\WGoose**.
8. Click on **OK** when the installation has been completed.

Installation Using the Program Disks (4)

1. Insert **Disk #1** in **Drive A** (or **Drive B**).
2. Click on **Start** in the Task Bar.
3. Click on **Run**.
4. At the text box, type **A:\SETUP** (or **B:\SETUP**)
5. Click on **OK**.
6. When prompted, Click on the **large icon** in the upper left corner of the dialogue box.
7. When prompted, insert **Disk #2** in **Drive A** (or **Drive B**). Click on **OK**.
8. When prompted, insert **Disk #3** in **Drive A** (or **Drive B**), then Click on **OK**.
9. When prompted, insert **Disk #4** in **Drive A** (or **Drive B**), then Click on **OK**.
10. Click on **OK** when the installation has been completed.

Creating the Data Disk:

To Run The Program, A Student Data Disk Must Be Created On A New, Blank, 3.5" High Density, Formatted Disk.

1. Click on **Start**, click on **Program**, then click on the **WGoose (sailboat) icon**.
2. Insert a **blank, 3.5" HD, formatted disk** in drive A or B. At the Disk Drive Verification Form, select the disk drive (**drive A or B**) containing the disk.
3. At the **Create Data Disk** form press the **Create Data Disk** command button.
4. When the disk is completed press the **Continue** command button.
5. At the **Disk Drive Verification Form**, click on **Quit**.
6. **Label your disk as WILD GOOSE DATA. Include your name and the date. You may wish to make a backup copy of your data disk.**

BEGIN THE PROGRAM
AND ENTER THE DATA

When you have: **(1) carefully read pages 1-11 of the Student Manual, (2) a good understanding of the accounts** used by Wild Goose Marina, Incorporated, **(3) completed the installation of the program, and, (4) prepared a new data disk,** as outlined on the previous page of this instruction sheet, you are ready to begin the journalizing process.

The transactions for your first work period (June 1st through 8th) begin on **page 18** of the Student Manual, and you are encouraged to prepare your account entry information before sitting down at the computer. This procedure will speed up your data entry time. An example of a written analysis for the first June 1 transaction is shown on **page 18**.

You may prefer to analyze each entry and record the transaction on the computer at the same time. You will be able to access the chart of accounts, customer list, and vendor list to the screen during the data entry process. This makes the recording of transactions and related information a very quick, easy, and efficient procedure.

TO BEGIN THE DATA ENTRY PROCESS, FOLLOW STEPS 1-5 AS OUTLINED BELOW:

1. Insert the Data Disk in Drive A (or Drive B).

2. From the Task Bar Click on Start.

3. Click on Programs, then Click on the WGoose (Sailboat) icon.

4. Select Drive A (or Drive B), Wait for verification, and then Click on Continue.

5 On the first run of the program You Must Enter Your Name (see instructions below)!

ENTER YOUR NAME and **check** it for **accuracy** (*it will be printed as entered on all documents*). Make any corrections necessary and then click on the **OK - Save Name** button. Your name is now encrypted on the data disk and all documents will be printed with your name and the date of the printing.

When the General Journal appears on the screen, click on the **Daily** Entries button. Read the narrative for the first June 1 transaction at the top of **page 18**. **Carefully follow instructions 1-6** as you begin the data entry procedure.

TRANSACTIONS FOR JUNE 1-8, 2001

June 1

Performed service and adjustment work on a Dolphin Houseboat and the customer paid cash for the work completed. The bill included $108.00 for 1.8 hours of labor ($60.00 per hour) plus sales tax (7%) of $7.56. The sales invoice number for this transaction is **W2130**.

101 115.56

412 108.00

211 7.56

<u>This transaction has not been recorded on the DATA disk! Click on the Daily entries button and follow instructions 1-6 below.</u>

1. *At the date prompt, enter 01 for June 1, and press the Enter key. When entering any part of the transaction, you may back up and reenter the information by using the backspace key. If the date has been entered incorrectly, click on the date prompt and reenter the date. You may also use the ERASE button to clear the entry at any time.*

2. *At the account prompt, type 101 and press the Enter or Tab key. To record the debit amount to the Cash account, enter $115.56 as the amount. Do not use dollar signs or commas for any entries. On this entry a decimal point is needed to separate the dollars and cents. If the account or the amount is incorrect, click on the appropriate item and reenter. Press the Enter or Tab key to move to the next position.*

3. *At the account prompt enter 412 and press the Enter or Tab key twice to move to the credit column. Enter $108.00 (without the dollar sign) as the credit to Service Fees Earned amount. Then enter 211 to record the credit to Sales Tax Payable and $7.56 as the amount.*

4. *When debits equal credits, the entry is complete. If any part of the journal entry is incorrect, click on the Erase button and reenter the transaction.*

5. *At the invoice number box enter W2130 as the sales invoice number. The alphabetic letter W may be entered in upper or lower case.*

6. *Check the entry carefully. If you wish to make a correction to the invoice number, click on the invoice box to clear it, and then enter the correct number. If the entry and all of the requested information is correct, click on the Post button.*

Continue entering the transactions for the first week. If you discover that a transaction entered into the system at an earlier time needs correction, **simply reverse or back out the error transaction and then enter the data correctly.** More detailed instructions on error correction procedures are given below. A complete summary of the error correction process begins on page 27.

TRANSACTIONS FOR JUNE 1-8, 2001

Student Analysis

FASTER DATA ENTRY USING THE "D" AND "C" KEYS!

June 1
Issued check number **01020** for $19.75. Invoice number **22344**
is to be charged to the Miscellaneous Expense account.

1. *Since this is another June 1 transaction, at the date prompt, enter D, and the June 1 date will be automatically entered for you. This saves data entry time when several transactions are recorded on the same date.*

2. *At the account prompt, enter 635 to record the debit to Miscellaneous Expense and enter $19.75 as the amount.*

3. *At the account prompt enter 101 and press the Enter or Tab key twice to move to the credit column. To automatically enter the credit amount press the C key and the credit amount will be entered for you.*

4. *At the check number text box enter check number 01020.*

5. *At the invoice number text box enter 22344.*

6. *Check the entry carefully. If the entry is correct, click on Post.*

∧∧∧

June 1
Discovered that the entry for payment of $19.75 for advertising
printing charges had been recorded in error to the Miscellaneous
Expense account rather than the Advertising Expense account.
This entry was recorded June 1 from invoice number **22344**.

1. *The entry correction procedure for the Wild Goose Marina accounting system requires that each error entry be backed out and then reentered correctly. Using the June 1 date for the error correction entries (press D for a repeat date), debit the Cash account and credit the Miscellaneous Expense account for the $19.75.*

2. *Again using the June 1 date, enter the second transaction correctly with a debit to Advertising Expense and a credit to Cash. When the check number prompt appears, enter ERROR to indicate that this is an error correction entry and a new check is not being issued. Enter the invoice number as requested. Additional error correction instructions are found on pages 27-28.*

    Note: This error correction procedure requires two journal entries, and leaves a clear audit trail of all corrections. This procedure is to be followed throughout this business simulation.

19

TRANSACTIONS FOR JUNE 1-8, 2001

June 1

Purchased on account from Luzzi, Incorporated, office supplies
listed at $119.00 and service and shop supplies totaling $676.00.
The invoice number is **L2556** and Luzzi offers net 10 cash terms.

Use the "C" key to automatically enter the credit amount to the Accounts Payable account.

1.   *Enter D to repeat the June 1 date.*

2.   *Enter account 129, Office Supplies, and the debit amount of $119.00.*

3.   *Enter account 131, Service and Shop Supplies, and the debit amount of $676.00.*

4.   *Enter account 201, Accounts Payable, and tab to the credit column. Press the "C" key and the credit amount will be automatically entered for you.*

    This feature may be used for both simple entries (one debit account and one credit account), and for compound journal entries at the last account credited.

5.   *At the invoice text box enter invoice L2556.*

6.   *At the vendor text box enter 24800 for Luzzi, Incorporated.*

∧∧

ACCOUNT SELECTION FROM THE CHART OF ACCOUNTS

June 1

Purchased **two** day cruiser pontoon boats from Snow Goose
Houseboats. The **list price** of the pontoon boats is $8,500 **each**
with a trade discount of **30%** The invoice number is **S3344**,
credit terms are net 30, and the boats are delivered by the seller.

1.   *Enter D to repeat the June 1 date.*

2.   *Click on the <u>Chart</u> of Accounts button.*

3.   *Click on account number 501 and the Purchases--Houseboats account will automatically be entered as a debit in the general journal. Enter the debit amount.*

4.   *Tab to the credit column and click again on the Chart button. Select account number 201 and the Accounts Payable account will appear. Press C and the credit amount will again be entered automatically.*

5.   *Enter the invoice number and the vendor number.*

6.   *Post to the general ledger.*

TRANSACTIONS FOR JUNE 1-8, 2001

June 1

Wild Goose Marina has $200,000 of Series One bonds outstanding. The bonds were sold November 30, 1999, (18 months ago) at a bond interest rate of 12% and a prevailing market interest rate of 11%. May 31 was the last day of the sixth bond interest quarter and the bond interest check (payable within three days of this date) must now be issued for $6,000 (check number **01021**). At the invoice prompt enter **INTPA** for interest payable.

An adjusting entry for bond interest and the amortization of bond premium was made at the end of the Wild Goose Marina first quarter, March 31 of this year. The adjusting entry recorded **1/3** of the expense and premium totals (one month) with a debit to Interest Expense for $1,876.33, a debit to Premium on Bonds Payable for $123.67, and a credit to Interest Payable for $2,000.00. This entry **was not reversed** at the beginning of this quarter (April 1).

Time Periods	Interest Paid	Interest Recognized	Amortization of Premium	Unamortized Premium	Carrying Amount of Bond
0				$6,402.29	$206,402.29
1	$6,000.00	$5,676.06	$323.94	6,078.35	206,078.35
2	6,000.00	5,667.15	332.85	5,745.50	205,745.50
3	6,000.00	5,658.00	342.00	5,403.50	205,403.50
4	6,000.00	5,648.60	351.40	5,052.10	205,052.10
5	6,000.00	5,638.93	361.07	4,691.03	204,691.03
6	6,000.00	5,629.00	371.00	4,320.03	204,320.03
7	6,000.00	5,618.80	381.20	3,938.83	203,938.83
8	6,000.00	5,608.32	391.68	3,547.15	203,547.15
9	6,000.00	5,597.55	402.45	3,144.70	203,144.70
10	6,000.00	5,586.48	413.52	2,731.18	202,731.18
11	6,000.00	5,575.11	424.89	2,306.29	202,306.29
12	6,000.00	5,563.42	436.58	1,869.71	201,869.71
13	6,000.00	5,551.42	448.58	1,421.13	201,421.13
14	6,000.00	5,539.08	460.92	960.21	200,960.21
15	6,000.00	5,526.41	473.59	486.62	200,486.62
16	6,000.00	5,513.38	486.62	0.00	0.00
Totals	$96,000.00	$89,597.71	$6,402.29		

^^

June 3

Sold a 55-foot, fully equipped Kruzer houseboat for **$147,500** cash plus **7%** sales tax. The sales invoice number is **W2131**. This deluxe unit includes the flying bridge, 225 HP V8, and generator.

21

TRANSACTIONS FOR JUNE 1-8, 2001

June 3
Issued check number **01022** and transferred $39,355.23 to the special payroll checking account. This entry clears the Salaries and Wages Payable account and transfers the exact amount of the wages and salaries to be paid with the distribution of the payroll checks on June 4. At the invoice prompt enter **PAYRL**.

∧∧

June 3
The market and bond interest rates have dropped significantly since the Series One bonds were issued. The Series One bonds ($200,000) are callable bonds and because the current interest rates are much lower than the rates that the company is currently paying, the bonds are retired today at a price of **103** (check number **01023**). At the invoice prompt type **RETIR**.

∧∧

June 4
Completed a spring tuneup and maintenance check on the two houseboats owned by Bettencourt, Inc., and billed the account for $1,550.43. This charge included $825 for service work, $624 for accessories and parts, and sales tax (sales invoice **W2132**). Remember that for this set sales tax is charged on all parts and service.

∧∧

June 4
Wild Goose Marina leases a hoist barge to assist in moving anchor blocks for the houseboat moorage stations. This lease is a five-year **operating lease** for equipment. The monthly rent of $1,500 is paid by the 4th of each month (check **01024**). At the invoice prompt typt **LRENT**.

TRANSACTIONS FOR JUNE 1-8, 2001

June 4
Received a check for $42,251.75 from Tisedaile Construction, Inc., as payment in full on account (sales invoice number **W2055**).

∧∧

June 5
Received a $6,500, 12.5%, 60-day note on account from Zakk, Incorporated, customer **11920**. The Zakk account is past due and the note was given by the customer to protect the credit line and demonstrate a positive intention to take care of the obligation. When the invoice number is requested, type **NTREC**.

∧∧

June 5
On April 3 of this year a 45-foot Kruzer Houseboat was sold to Brad Jones and Company. The total selling price was $96,500 with a down payment of $26,500 and an installment note receivable for $70,000 calling for monthly payments of **$10,000** plus **12% interest** (calculated monthly) on the unpaid balance. Received the **second payment check** from this customer. The original sales invoice was **W1901**.

∧∧

June 5
Issued check number **01025** in payment of all cash dividends. The 10,000 shares of $20 par value preferred stock (8% non-cumulative, non-participating) will receive a 2.0% quarterly dividend. The 20,000 shares of common stock will receive $1.08 per share. The dividends were declared on May 10, and are payable today, June 5. The share totals shown for each class of stock are the number of shares outstanding on May 31, the date of record. At the invoice prompt enter **DVPAY**.

23

TRANSACTIONS FOR JUNE 1-8, 2001

June 6

Acquired, on a special purchase basis, new shop equipment for cleaning and sealing pontoons (invoice number **X2990**). The manufacturer will sell Wild Goose Marina the equipment with no down payment, monthly payment, or interest charges. The only obligation of Wild Goose Marina will be to work with the seller's personnel if there are any equipment problems and to make a lump-sum payment (secured by a non-interest bearing, long-term note) of $25,000, three years from today. The prevailing interest rate for this type of transaction is 14%. **Use Table A (Present Value) in the appendix to determine the cost basis of the shop equipment.**

^^

June 6

In anticipation of a possible short-term cash problem, discounted a $140,000, 14%, 90-day, note receivable dated May 2. A 12% discount rate is charged by the lender (use exact days and a 360-day banker's year). At the invoice prompt type **DISNT** for discounted note.

^^

June 7

Issued check **01026** as payment in full on invoice **K2244** from Kruzer Houseboats. The invoice dated May 28 totals $260,000 with terms of 2/10, n30.

^^

June 7

The $550.00 account balance of customer Dale Novice has proven to be uncollectible and is written off. Wild Goose Marina uses the **allowance method** for all bad debt write-offs. When the invoice number is requested type **WROFF**.

24

TRANSACTIONS FOR JUNE 1-8, 2001

June 8
Check number **01027** is issued to pay all federal income taxes withheld and all FICA taxes withheld, as well as paid for the employees, for the month of May. At the invoice prompt enter **FEDTX** for federal taxes.

You may check the balances due by listing the current trial balance (click on the General Ledger tab) or by checking the May 31, 2001 trial balance in the appendix of this handbook.

∧∧

June 8
Sold 1,000 shares of $100 par value common stock to a stockholder at the current market price of $130.50 per share. At the invoice prompt type **CSTOK** for common stock.

∧∧

June 8
Received a cash dividend of $.42 (42 cents) per share on the 10,000 shares of Granite Bay Jet Ski, Corporation, common stock held as a short-term investment. At the invoice prompt type **DVREC** for dividend received.

∧∧

June 8
Received a $122,250 check as the second and **final installment** on the common stock subscription signed in March. Issued the shares to the subscriber. The subscription was for 2,000 shares of $100 par value common stock at $122.25 per share and a cash deposit was received at that time for 50% of the subscription contract. At the invoice prompt type **SUBRE** for subscriptions receivable. *Two entries are required to complete this transaction.*

Now that you have completed entering the transactions for the first week, June 1-8, it is time to check the accuracy of your work.

1. *Click on the General Ledger Tab.*

2. *Click on the printer icon and print the Trial Balance.*

3. *Compare your Trial Balance totals with the "Check It Out" box at the bottom of this page. Remember that accounts with zero balances will not appear on the Trial Balance.*

"CHECK IT OUT"

101 Cash	. . . .	$ 282,363.56
105 Accounts Receivable	. . . .	83,370.43
106 Allowance for Doubtful Accounts	. . . .	1,967.00
129 Office Supplies	. . . .	1,362.00
145 Service & Shop Equipment	. . . .	205,395.00
201 Accounts Payable	. . . .	30,995.00
202 Interest Payable	. . . .	0.00
208 Common Cash Dividends Payable	. . . .	0.00
209 Salaries & Wages Payable	. . . .	0.00
211 Sales Tax Payable	. . . .	28,276.69
223 FICA Taxes Payable	. . . .	0.00
242 Discount on Long-Term Notes Payable	. . . . . .	8,125.00
252 Premium on Bonds Payable	. . . .	0.00
305 Common Stock	. . . .	2,300,000.00
306 Common Stock Subscribed	. . . .	0.00
401 Houseboat Sales	. . . .	1,052,000.00
407 Accessories & Parts Sales	. . . .	37,957.00
502 Purchases Discounts--Houseboats	. . . .	14,600.00
604 Equipment Rental Expense	. . . .	4,500.00
711 Interest Earned	. . . .	7,044.69
713 Dividends Earned	. . . .	6,511.00
813 Interest Expense	. . . .	13,877.67
825 Loss on Retirement of Bonds	. . . .	1,679.97
TRIAL BALANCE	. . . .	$4,318,771.04

IF ALL OF YOUR TOTALS MATCH THE CHECK FIGURES, you are ready to enter the transactions for the second week of June or exit the system and complete the work for module 2 at a later time. **If any of your figures do not match the "Check It Out" block, print a copy of the general journal.** From the General Journal Tab, click on the **Print/View Icon** in the **Tool Bar.** When the journal entries appear, click on **First Week,** then click on the **Print Icon.** Then click on **Close.** Be sure to use the error correction procedures outlined on pages 27 and 28 to correct all errors.

For **accuracy, efficiency,** and **a clear audit trail,** use ONLY the correction system designed for the Wild Goose Marina, Inc., accounting system. Any account that is not correct is a major clue for you to check out. **Your account balances must match the check figures.**

For error tracking it is also possible to view or print all general ledger accounts, all accounts receivable and accounts payable subsidiary ledger accounts.

All documents for June 8 must be printed and corrected BEFORE TRANSACTIONS FOR THE SECOND WORK PERIOD ARE RECORDED. Additional entries will change the account balances and the Trial Balance totals for June 8 will not be stored for recall at a later time.

ERROR CORRECTION PROCEDURES

For the Wild Goose Marina Accounting System

JOURNAL ENTRY CORRECTION

Carefully examine all entries recorded for each period and when an error is found use the following correction procedure:

1. Back the transaction out using the date used in the error entry.

2. Enter the correct transaction using the correct date of the original entry.

If, for example, you find that you entered a cash sales transaction for June 3 without recording the sales tax, simply back out (**reverse**) the error as follows:

| *June 3* | *Service Fees Earned* | 350.00 | |
| | *Cash* | | 350.00 |

Enter **ERROR** at the check number prompt since this is a **correction** to cash and **does not** involve the issuance of another check.

Using the same June 3 date, record the correct entry.

June 3	*Cash*	378.00	
	Service Fees Earned		350.00
	Sales Tax Payable		28.00

The error entry, the backout entry, and the correction entry will appear in the accounting records leaving a clear, easy-to-follow audit trail.

When the account balances match those in the **"Check It Out"** block, you are ready to enter the transactions for the next period. If you are finished entering transactions for this session, exit the system.

WILD GOOSE MARINA, INCORPORATED

TRANSACTIONS

FOR

JUNE 9 - 15

TRANSACTIONS FOR JUNE 9-15, 2001

June 9

Sold, on consignment for a customer, the used houseboat moored at station 99. The selling price of the houseboat was $49,500. The standard commission of 8% on the first $20,000 and 2% on the balance above $20,000 was earned on this sale. At the invoice prompt type **CE601**.

∧∧

June 9

Sold 1,500 shares of Folsom Corporation common stock held as a short-term investment. The stock sold for 19-1/4, less a commission of $192.50. The stock was originally purchased for $17,925.50. At the invoice prompt type **STOKS**.

∧∧

June 9

Billed Kingston & Sons, Inc., $5,350 for a houseboat pull-out, pontoon repair, and pontoon sealing, $750 for parts and accessories, and sales tax on the total (invoice **W2133**).

∧∧

June 9

Donated, to the Lincoln Hills High School Auto Shop Class, a used pickup truck that is no longer being used. The old truck originally cost $5,950, has no current **market value**, and a book value of $200. The asset was fully depreciated to salvage value ($200 value) at the end of the first quarter, March 31, 2001. At the invoice prompt type **DONAT**.

∧∧

June 10

Received a check for $432 from J. P. Elam as payment in full on account. The balance due was written off as uncollectible on April 10 of this year after all attempts for collection had failed. **Two entries are required** to update this account. At the invoice prompt type **RECOV**.

TRANSACTIONS FOR JUNE 9-15, 2001

June 10
Issued check **01028** for $735 to Houseboating Fun magazine for additional advertising (invoice **HF244**).

∧∧

June 11
Issued check **01029** to Corr Marine Supply for parts and accessories purchased May 27 (invoice **C6211**). The items were listed at $15,812.50, with a trade discount of 20%, and terms of 1/15, n30.

∧∧

June 11
Declared a **1% stock dividend** on the 23,000 shares of common stock ($100 par value) that are currently outstanding. The closing price of the stock today is $125.00 per share. The date of record will be June 15 and the stocks will be issued on June 25. At the invoice prompt type **STKDV**.

∧∧

June 11
Issued check number **01030** to Luzzi, Inc., as payment in full of invoice **L2556**. The original purchase of supplies on June 1 totaled $795.00, and carried net 10 terms. There have been no returns on this order.

∧∧

June 12
Sales Manager, Al Price has resigned and is taking a job with another firm. Purchased back 300 shares of common stock from Al at an agreed-upon price of $135.25 per share (check number **01031**). These shares are treasury shares and **will not be retired**. At the invoice prompt type **TSTOK**.

31

TRANSACTIONS FOR JUNE 9-15, 2001

June 12

Sold old office equipment for $325 cash. The equipment originally cost $950 and depreciation to March 31 of this year (the end of the first quarter) totals $825. The asset depreciates on a straight-line basis at a rate of $25 per month and depreciation is calculated **to the nearest month.** At the invoice prompt for the depreciation entry type **DEPRE**. At the invoice prompt for the sale of the equipment type **ASALE** (asset sale). Two entries are required.

^^^

June 13

Service work totaling $2,450, plus sales tax, was performed on the houseboat moored at station 204 (invoice **W2134**). The customer paid the full amount due with a cashiers check.

^^^

June 13

Sold a houseboat canopy to J. P. Elam for $3,650, plus installation service fees of $550, and sales tax. Mr. Elam paid in full with a check (invoice **W2135**).

^^^

June 13

Purchased office supplies on account from Rockwood Business Supply (terms net 30). The total charge of $566.22 (taxes included) is listed on invoice number **55663**.

^^^

June 13

Received a cash dividend of $.62 (62 cents) per share on the 1,000 shares of Ramblewood Manufacturing common stock held as a short-term investment. Ramblewood does a major share of the steel and welding work for the marina. At the invoice prompt type **DVREC**.

TRANSACTIONS FOR JUNE 9-15, 2001

June 14
Returned office supplies with a total value of $28.25 (tax included) to Rockwood Business Supply. The office supplies were purchased on account June 13 (invoice number **55663**).

^^

June 14
Issued a credit memo (**CM201**) to R. J. Corsetti, customer 10820, and credited his account $192.60 (tax included) for a $180.00 overcharge on service work completed on his houseboat (invoice **W2095**). The final billing of May 17 had been calculated in error.

^^

June 14
Received notice from the bank that the $4,494 check received from J. P. Elam as payment for merchandise and services (invoice **W2135**) has not cleared for lack of funds. The balance of this NSF check **and an additional company handling fee of $40** will be charged back to the J. P. Elam account. The **handling fee charged will be entered as Miscellaneous Revenue**. At the check number prompt type **BADCK**.

^^

June 15
Shipped a replacement part (at no charge) to a customer at Eagle Lake. Paid the delivery charges by issuing check number **01032** for $27.50 to Quickenback Delivery Service (invoice **Q1521**).

^^

June 15
Instead of a costly "patch up" repair expense to the heavy duty truck used to pull the special houseboat trailer, the truck engine and drive train are completely rebuilt. The cost of this major overhaul is $8,790 and is paid in full with check number **01033**. This **extraordinary repair** will **extend the useful life** of the machine to four years. At the invoice prompt type **EXTRA**.

TRANSACTIONS FOR JUNE 9-15, 2001

June 15

Series Two Bonds with a face value of $400,000 are sold and issued today by Wild Goose Marina. The bonds carry a 7.0% interest rate and are sold at a price to yield an annual return of 8.0% to the investor. The 5-year bonds will pay quarterly interest on the 15th of September, December, March and June. At the invoice prompt type **BONDS**. **Use the appropriate present value factors from Table B in the appendix to complete the necessary calculations.**

∧∧∧

June 15

Cash receipts for moorage fees received by Wild Goose Marina during the past 15 days total $12,330. These receipts have been properly credited to customer accounts in the moorage log and properly deposited in the cash account, but have not yet been recorded in the General Journal. Total moorage fees earned during the quarter will be accounted for in the adjusting entry process. At the invoice prompt type **MF061**.

∧∧∧

June 15

Issued check **01034** for $31,500 to the IRS as the second installment payment for income taxes. At the invoice prompt type **INCTX**.

∧∧∧

THIS COMPLETES THE WORK FOR THE SECOND PERIOD ENDING JUNE 15. IT IS NOW TIME TO CHECK THE ACCURACY OF YOUR WORK.

1. Click on the General Ledger Tab.

2. Click on the Printer Icon and print the Trial Balance.

3. Check your Trial Balance totals with the accounts and balances found in the "Check It Out" box on the next page.

```
                        "CHECK IT OUT"

    101 Cash . . . . . . . . . . . . . . . . . . . $  618,278.36
    103 Short-Term Investments . . . . . . . . . .    124,091.50
    105 Accounts Receivable . . . . . . . . . . . .    94,238.83
    106 Allowance for Doubtful Accounts . . . . . .     2,399.00
    129 Office Supplies . . . . . . . . . . . . . . .    1,899.97
    150 Accumulated Depreciation, Trucks . . . .      13,710.00
    201 Accounts Payable . . . . . . . . . . . . .     18,087.97
    211 Sales Tax Payable . . . . . . . . . . . . .    29,156.59
    215 Unearned Moorage Fees . . . . . . . . . .      84,880.00
    251 Discount on Bonds Payable . . . . . . . .      16,340.20
    307 Common Stock Dividends Distributable . .       23,000.00
    325 Stock Dividends Declared . . . . . . . . .     28,750.00
    330 Treasury Stock . . . . . . . . . . . . . .     40,575.00
    407 Accessories & Parts Sales . . . . . . . . .    42,357.00
    412 Service Fees Earned . . . . . . . . . . . .    47,218.00
    502 Purchases Discounts--Houseboats . . . . .      14,600.00
    608 Advertising Expense . . . . . . . . . . . .     3,004.75
    609 Credit Card Expense . . . . . . . . . . . . .      295.21
    610 Delivery Expense . . . . . . . . . . . . . . .       89.62
    713 Dividends Earned . . . . . . . . . . . . . .     7,131.00
    721 Gain on Sale of Assets . . . . . . . . . . .     1,500.00
    741 Miscellaneous Revenue . . . . . . . . . . . .       96.00
    811 Income Taxes Expense . . . . . . . . . . .     31,500.00
    821 Loss on Sale/Disposal of Assets . . . . . . .      250.00
    TRIAL BALANCE . . . . . . . . . . . . . . .   $4,759,444.41
```

If any of your figures do not match the "Check It Out" block, print a copy of **the general journal.** From the General Journal Tab, click on the **Print/View Icon** in the **Tool Bar**. When the journal entries appear, click on **Second Week**, then click on the **Print Icon**. Then click on **Close**. Be sure to use the error correction procedures outlined on pages 27 and 28 to correct all errors.

When your totals match the check figures above, print the following documents:

1. **Print the following General Ledger Accounts. Click on the Ledger Account Icon and <u>print the Cash account that appears on the screen</u>** (account 101).

From the ledger selection box select and print the following <u>additional</u> General Ledger accounts:

    105 Accounts Receivable
    106 Allowance for Doubtful Accounts
    201 Accounts Payable
    330 Treasury Stock
    412 Service Fees Earned
    713 Dividends Earned

2. Print the Schedule of Accounts Receivable. Click on the Subsidiary Ledgers Tab, Click on the Print View Icon and print the Schedule of Accounts Receivable.

3. Print the Accounts Receivable Subsidiary Ledger. Click on the Print All Icon and print the Accounts Receivable Subsidiary Ledger.

4. Print the Schedule of Accounts Payable. Click on the Accounts Payable View Schedule Icon. Click on the Print View Icon and print the Schedule of Accounts Payable.

5. Print the Accounts Payable Subsidiary Ledger. Click on the Print All Icon and print the Accounts Payable Subsidiary Ledger.

Using all of your printed documents, answer the questions on the Mid-Project Evaluation forms.

BE SURE TO PRINT ALL OF YOUR DOCUMENTS <u>BEFORE</u> CONTINUING THE JOURNALIZING PROCESS FOR JUNE 16-22!

MID-PROJECT EVALUATION

WILD GOOSE MARINA INCORPORATED

June 15, 2001

MID-PROJECT EVALUATION

WILD GOOSE MARINA, INCORPORATED

NAME_____

SECTION_____DATE_____

1. Do the balances on your printed Trial Balance match the amounts shown in the **"Check It Out"** block?

   YES_____NO_____

2. What was the *correct* balance of the Cash account at the close of business on June 9?

   $_____

3. What invoice was paid in full with check number 01026 on June 7?

   Invoice Number_____

4. What was the correct balance of the Accounts Receivable account after the first accounts receivable entry of June 4?

   $_____

5-6. An entry for $1,550.43 was debited to the Accounts Receivable account on June 4. Which customer was involved in this transaction (identify by number) and what was the sales invoice number?

   Customer Number_____

   Invoice Number_____

7. An entry for $6,500.00 was credited to the Accounts Receivable account on June 5. What was the reason for this credit?

   _____

8. At the close of business on June 11, what was the correct balance of the Accounts Payable account?

   $_____

9-10. On June 11, an entry for $12,650.00 was debited to the Accounts Payable account. Identify the name of the vendor/creditor and the number of the invoice paid.

   Vendor/Creditor Name_____

   Invoice Number_____

11. When the Treasury Stock account has a normal balance does it *increase* or *decrease* the value of the stockholders' equity?

   _____

12. How much was earned in Service Fees on June 13?

   $_____

13. Why was the Service Fees account debited on June 14?

   _____

14. What is the total amount of dividends earned that had been reported as of the close of business June 8?

   $_____

15. On June 14, which customer has the largest outstanding balance?

   Customer Number_____

MID-PROJECT EVALUATION
WILD GOOSE MARINA, INCORPORATED

16. Explain the activity in the J. P. Elam account on June 10. _____

17-18. Which customer was issued credit memo CM201 and what was the account balance after the credit to the customer's account?

Customer Number_____

$_____

19. Customer accounts are due 30 days after the invoice date. Carefully examine the Accounts Receivable subsidiary ledger. Identify by name the customer whose account is past due.

Customer Name_____

20. Why does the Dale Novice account now have a $0.00 balance? _____

21. Before the June 4 entry, what was the balance of the Tisedaile Construction Company account?

$_____

22. Does the balance of the Schedule of Accounts Receivable match the balance of the Accounts Receivable account?

YES_____NO_____

23. If financial statements were prepared as of June 14, what would be the reported **Net** Accounts Receivable balance?

$_____

24. What terms are extended by the Corr Marine Supply? _____

25. What was the balance of the Corr Marine Supply accounts payable account before payment of June 11?

$_____

26. Which accounts payable account is past due and should have been paid within ten days to earn the discount.

Vendor Number _____

27. Which current accounts payable account is the next to be paid?

Vendor Number _____

28. What amount of cash was required to pay off the Kruzer Houseboats account balance on June 7?

$_____

29. Explain the reason for the $28.25 reduction in the balance owed to Rockwood Business Supply.

_____

30. On what date is the balance owed to Rockwood Business Supply due and payable?

Date_____

31. What has been the net amount of increase in all forms of long-term debt since the May 31 Trial Balance?

$_____

32. What is the total amount of contributed capital on June 15?

$_____

33. Net Accessories & Parts Sales are what percent of total <u>Net</u> <u>Sales</u> as of June 15, the end of the second week?

_____%

34-35. What has been the total increase or decrease in the carrying value (net liability) of bonds payable since the May 31 Trial Balance?

$_____

Increase/Decrease_____

WILD GOOSE MARINA, INCORPORATED

TRANSACTIONS

FOR

JUNE 16-22

TRANSACTIONS FOR JUNE 16-22, 2001

June 16

Issued check **01035** for $972 in payment of legal services for the legal team of Sanchez and Sanchez (invoice **SS255**).

^^

June 16

Purchased 500 shares of stock in SunKraft Houseboats at 14 5/8 plus a commission of $115.50 (check **01036**). This will be treated as a long-term investment. At the invoice prompt enter **INVST**.

^^

June 17

Sold to a company executive 100 shares of Treasury Stock at a price of $142.25 per share. The stock had been purchased for $135.25 per share on June 12. At the invoice prompt enter **TSTOK**.

^^

June 17

State sales tax collected through the end of the work day June 15 is now due and payable and must be forwarded to the State Board of Equalization. At the invoice prompt enter **SALTX**. Check **01037** is issued to pay this obligation. (Check the June 15 Trial Balance or the General Ledger.)

TRANSACTIONS FOR JUNE 16-22, 2001

June 17
Purchased new houseboats from Kruzer Houseboats. The invoice (number **K3556**) lists the houseboats at $439,500 and freight charges (FOB shipping point) to the launching ramp totaling $19,500. Kruzer offers terms of 2/10, n/30 on all **houseboats**.

∧∧

June 17
Sold a 32-foot pontoon boat and 90-hp motor (**Service & Shop Equipment**) for $2,600 cash. This boat was used extensively to ferry customers, haul equipment, and to provide service work to houseboats. The package was purchased at a cost of $8,600 and on March 31, the end of first quarter, had depreciated $7,500. The salvage value of the unit is $500, and straight-line depreciation is $100 per month ($300 per quarter). At the invoice prompt for the update of the depreciation enter **DEPRE** for depreciation. At the invoice prompt for the sale of the boat, enter **ASALE** for asset sale.

∧∧

June 18
Received a cashiers check for $4,534.00 and a letter of apology from J. P. Elam. The check is to cover a NSF check that was received on June 13 as payment of invoice **W2135** and charged back to Mr. Elam's account on June 14.

∧∧

June 18
Issued check **01038** for $278.50 to Spotless Office Janitorial Service for cleaning services received (invoice number **12655**).

TRANSACTIONS FOR JUNE 16-22, 2001

June 19

The uncollectible balance for Taylor Company is $2,670. Received a check for $1,670.00 from a bank trustee as final settlement of a bankruptcy claim against Taylor Company. At the invoice prompt enter **WROFF**.

^^

June 19

Jason Phillips, a major investor in Wild Goose Marina, has subscribed for an additional 1,200 shares of $100 par value common stock at $135.00 per share. A check for 30% of the total purchase price of the stock is received today along with the signed subscription agreement. The balance of the cash will be received in 45 days. At the invoice prompt enter **SUBRE**. **(Two entries required.)**

^^

June 19

Issued check **01039** for $1,215 to Hisinger & Reed Insurance Agency for additional liability coverage (invoice number **HR651**).

^^

June 19

On April 20 of this year Wild Goose Marina, Inc., borrowed cash by discounting a $90,000, 60-day, note payable. The lender charged a 11% discount fee and the Interest Expense account was debited for $1,650. Proceeds of $88,350 were received and deposited in the Cash account. This note is due today and is paid in full with check **01040**. At the invoice prompt enter **DISNT**.

^^

June 20

Issued check **01041** for $83.75 for the purchase of additional tools (invoice **11334**).

TRANSACTIONS FOR JUNE 16-22, 2001

June 20
Purchased houseboat generators and flood lights on account from Yee and Associates (terms net 30 and goods shipped FOB destination). The merchandise lists for $13,125 with **trade discounts** of **35%** and **5%**. The invoice number for this purchase is **T3555**.

ΛΛΛΛΛΛΛΛΛΛΛΛΛΛΛΛΛΛΛΛΛΛΛΛΛΛΛΛΛΛΛΛΛΛΛΛΛΛΛΛΛΛΛΛΛΛΛΛΛ

June 21
Sold a 60-foot Super Kruzer Houseboat and received a check from the customer for $223,500.00. Sales invoice **W2136** lists the houseboat selling price plus sales tax of $14,621.50.

ΛΛΛΛΛΛΛΛΛΛΛΛΛΛΛΛΛΛΛΛΛΛΛΛΛΛΛΛΛΛΛΛΛΛΛΛΛΛΛΛΛΛΛΛΛΛΛΛ

June 21
Wild Goose Marina, Inc., owns 30% of Baldwin Manufacturing, Inc., and, as a substantial investor, has a significant influence over the operations of this company. All earnings from this investment are accounted for using the **equity method**. Baldwin has just completed their fiscal year as of May 31 and has today officially notified all stockholders of an after tax net income of $56,500. At the invoice prompt enter **EARNS**.

ΛΛΛΛΛΛΛΛΛΛΛΛΛΛΛΛΛΛΛΛΛΛΛΛΛΛΛΛΛΛΛΛΛΛΛΛΛΛΛΛΛΛΛΛΛΛΛΛ

June 22
Completed a major pullout and pontoon sealing job on the four houseboats owned by Roseburg & Associates. Billed the Roseburg account for service work and sales tax totaling $14,338 (sales invoice **W2137**). Hint: Divide by 1.07.

TRANSACTIONS FOR JUNE 16-22, 2001

June 22

Traded the old four-wheel drive cable truck for a new truck issuing check number **01042** to complete the transaction. The old truck cost $12,600 (**salvage value $2,000**) and on March 31, the end of the first quarter, had depreciated $9,000. Straight-line depreciation on the old truck is $250 per month (use **DEPRE** at the invoice prompt).

The new truck sells for an out-the-door price of $34,500 (invoice **N1566**) and Sierra Truck Sales is allowing a $4,500 trade-in allowance on the purchase of the new vehicle. The IRS method (no gains or losses recognized) is used when recording all trades.

An additional check (number **01043**) for $695.50 was issued to the Department of Motor Vehicles (invoice **DMV06**) for the vehicle license and registration fees.

Three entries are required for this trade.

∧∧∧

June 22

Issued check number **01044** for $75,000 to Granite Bay Concrete for leasehold improvements made to the launching ramp and parking areas (**G7777**).

∧∧∧

When all of the transactions for the week have been entered, call the trial balance to the screen and check your account totals against the figures in the **"Check It Out"** block. If all of your totals match the check figures, you are ready to enter the transactions for the period of June 23-30. If your totals do not match the check figures, carefully check the journal entries, locate the error/s, and enter the necessary correction/s. **Remember, the most efficient way to locate errors is to print a copy of the General Journal and the Trial Balance!**

"CHECK IT OUT"

101	Cash	$ 678,578.02
105	Accounts Receivable	101,372.83
106	Allowance for Doubtful Accounts	1,399.00
116	Subscriptions Receivable, Common Stock	113,400.00
140	Investment in Baldwin Manufacturing	224,509.70
141	Long-Term Investments	1,257,428.00
146	Accumulated Depre., Service & Shop Equip	32,855.00
149	Trucks	62,850.00
201	Accounts Payable	485,192.66
203	Short-Term Notes Payable	0.00
211	Sales Tax Payable	15,559.50
305	Common Stock	2,300,000.00
308	Cont. Capital in Excess of Par, Common	128,250.00
330	Treasury Stock	27,050.00
401	Houseboat Sales	1,260,878.50
503	Transportation-In--Houseboats	32,605.00
611	Tools Expense	170.25
615	Depreciation Expense, Trucks	750.00
715	Earnings on Investments	16,950.00
721	Gain on Sale of Assets	3,300.00
	TRIAL BALANCE	$5,509,180.51

WILD GOOSE MARINA, INCORPORATED

TRANSACTIONS

FOR

JUNE 23 - 30

TRANSACTIONS FOR JUNE 23-30,

June 23

Purchased on account from Quinlivin, Incorporated, supplies for the shop that list at $136.00 and tools that list for $47.00. Sales tax on this asset acquisition totals $12.81. Assign the sales tax properly to each asset or expense account and record the entry (invoice number **Q3456**). Quinlivin extends net 30 terms.

∧∧

June 24

Received a $19,000, 13%, 90-day, note receivable from Adams Farms, Incorporated, as payment in full on account. The original invoice is dated May 25 and the sales invoice number is **W2115**.

∧∧

June 24

Issued check **01045** and retired 50% of the Preferred Stock. The $20 par value stock (10,000 shares) sold originally for $22 per share. The stock is retired for $21.75 per share (**RSTOK**). This is the first retirement of any stock for Wild Goose Marina, Inc.

∧∧

June 25

Issued check number **01046** to Bidwell Truck Service for truck gas and repairs totaling $563.80 (invoice **66555**).

TRANSACTIONS FOR JUNE 23-30, 2001

June 25
Issued, to the stockholders of record of June 15, the 230 shares declared in the June 11 stock dividend. At the invoice prompt enter **STKDV**.

∧∧∧

June 26
Sold the used houseboat moored at station 137. Earned and received the standard commission (8% on the first $20,000, 2% on the balance above $20,000) on the selling price of $85,500. At the invoice prompt type **CE602**.

∧∧

June 26
Traded an old forklift (Service & Shop Equipment) for a new heavy-duty forklift issuing check number **01047**. The old forklift cost $4,950 and on March 31 had depreciated $2,600. Units-of-production depreciation is used for the forklift and 25 cents per hour is the depreciation rate. The hour meter shows 120.0 hours of use since the end of last quarter. At the invoice prompt enter **DEPRE**.

The new forklift lists for $40,000 (**invoice X3355**), and a $2,800 trade-in allowance on the old forklift is given by the seller. The IRS method is used for recording all trades. Two entries are required for this transaction.

∧∧

June 26
Issued the following checks as payment in full for miscellaneous billings:

> Check **01048** to PG&E for utilities (electric and gas) totaling $436.50 (invoice **14388**).

> Check **01049** to Shasta Valley Telephone for $399.80 (invoice **2555T**).

TRANSACTIONS FOR JUNE 23-30, 2001

June 27
Issued check **01050** and paid in full the **June 17** invoice (**K3556**) from Kruzer Houseboats

^^^

June 28
Purchased for resale two Model 70 Daycruiser Houseboats paying $30,000 cash (check **01051**) as a down payment and issuing a $160,000, 90-day, 12% note payable for the balance (invoice number **46005**).

^^^

June 28
Received $106,975 cash by issuing a $110,000, non-interest bearing, 90-day Note Payable. The lender discounted the note charging a 11% discount fee. Remember that the 360-day banker's year is used in calculating interest. *Because of the timing of this note, the lender discount will be debited to the appropriate Discount on Notes Payable account.* At the invoice prompt enter **NTPAY**.

^^^

June 28
Issued check **01052** as payment in full of the <u>**May 29**</u>, $5,650 invoice from Foster Business Supply. Terms extended by Foster are 2/10, n/30 and the invoice number is **F1466**.

^^^

June 29
Issued check **01053** for $5,625 to Gold Country Freight as payment in full for delivery of the two Daycruiser Houseboats to the launching ramp (invoice **G4411**).

TRANSACTIONS FOR JUNE 23-30, 2001

June 29
Issued check **01054** to replenish the $100 Petty Cash fund. A total of **$54.50** remains in the petty cash box at this time. Be sure to account for any overage or shortage in the fund. A summary of receipts (**PC601**) lists the following expenditures made from petty cash:

Office Supplies	$10.50
Miscellaneous Expense	17.50
Delivery Expense	16.50

∧∧

June 29
A completed bank reconciliation notes the following items requiring journal entries:

> **Collection of a $5,550, 12%, 6-month note receivable**
> At the invoice prompt enter **NTREC**.

> **Interest Earned on the Checking Account $67.50**
> At the invoice prompt enter **BKINT**.

> *Two journal entries are required.*

∧∧

June 30
A cash dividend check is received today from Baldwin Manufacturing. Baldwin Manufacturing declared a cash dividend on June 21 for $20,000, payable to all stockholders on June 29. (Check the June 21 transaction for additional information). At the invoice prompt enter **INVST**.

∧∧

June 30
Sold 400 shares of Glitch Company stock for 4 3/8 ($4.375) per share less a commission of $52. The shares were held as a short-term investment. The shares were purchased earlier for $10 per share plus a commission of $92. At the invoice prompt enter **INVST**.

TRANSACTIONS FOR JUNE 23-30, 2001

June 30
Issued check **01055** to the Delta Equipment Company. Wild Goose Marina, Inc., has a long-term note obligation with Delta that calls for a quarterly principal payment of $10,000, plus 10.5% interest on the unpaid balance. This obligation was initiated exactly one year ago with the purchase of service and shop equipment for $120,000. Three payments have been made to date. At the invoice prompt enter **NTPAY**.

∧∧

June 30
Record the payroll for the month of June from the payroll information listed below. At the invoice prompt enter **PAYRL**. Cash for the payroll will be transferred to the special payroll checking account on July 1 and the payroll checks will be issued **July 2**.

Gross Earnings:

Office & Shop Wages & Salaries	$36,088.77
Executive and Sales Salaries	18,000.00

Taxes withheld and payable:

Employee Income Taxes Payable	$7,444.55

FICA (Social Security & Medicare) Taxes Payable total 7.65 percent of the total gross earnings of all employees (round to the nearest cent). As of June 30, no employees have reached the ceiling for Social Security or Medicare.

∧∧

June 30
Employer payroll taxes require a matching of the employee's FICA contribution. The State (**2.4%**) and Federal (**.8%**) Unemployment Tax obligations on this payroll must also be recorded. For the June payroll, $11,545.00 of employee earnings are below the ceiling and are taxable for Federal and State Unemployment taxes. At the invoice prompt enter **EMTAX**.

These tax liabilities will be paid to the appropriate tax entities in early July.

TRANSACTIONS FOR JUNE 23-30, 2001

June 30

One year ago on June 30, 2000, a **capital lease** for service and shop equipment was signed with Medford Equipment Company. The agreement called for sixteen quarterly lease payments of $500 to be paid the last working day of each quarter for the next four years. On the date the contract was signed the prevailing interest rate was 10% and the journal entry included debits to Service and Shop Equipment for $6,527.50 and Discount On Lease Financing for $1,472.50. The equipment will become the property of the lessee at the end of the lease period. The **interest method** is used to amortize the Discount on Lease Financing and the amount to be amortized for the quarter totals $137.29. The chart below presents the results of the interest calculations for each of the sixteen quarters. At the invoice prompt enter **LEASE**.

Two entries are required.

1. Issue check **01056** for the quarterly lease payment.

2. Amortize the Discount on Lease Financing for the quarter.

Quarterly depreciation on this asset will be recorded as a part of the adjusting entries.

Lease Payment per Quarter	$500.00
Term of Lease in Quarters	16
Prevailing Annual Interest Rate	10.00%

Time Period	Beginning Of Quarter Lease Liability	Beginning Of Quarter Unamortized Discount	Beginning Of Quarter Carrying Amount	Discount To Be Amortized	End Of Quarter Lease Liability	End Of Quarter Unamortized Discount
1	$8,000.00	$1,472.50	$6,527.50	$163.19	$7,500.00	$1,309.31
2	7,500.00	1,309.31	6,190.69	154.77	7,000.00	1,154.54
3	7,000.00	1,154.54	5,845.46	146.14	6,500.00	1,008.41
4	6,500.00	1,008.41	5,491.59	137.29	6,000.00	871.12
5	6,000.00	871.12	5,128.88	128.22	5,500.00	742.90
6	5,500.00	742.90	4,757.10	118.93	5,000.00	623.97
7	5,000.00	623.97	4,376.03	109.40	4,500.00	514.57
8	4,500.00	514.57	3,985.43	99.64	4,000.00	414.93
9	4,000.00	414.93	3,585.07	89.63	3,500.00	325.30
10	3,500.00	325.30	3,174.70	79.37	3,000.00	245.94
11	3,000.00	245.94	2,754.06	68.85	2,500.00	177.09
12	2,500.00	177.09	2,322.91	58.07	2,000.00	119.01
13	2,000.00	119.01	1,880.99	47.02	1,500.00	71.99
14	1,500.00	71.99	1,428.01	35.70	1,000.00	36.29
15	1,000.00	36.29	963.71	24.09	500.00	12.20
16	500.00	12.20	487.80	12.20	0.00	0.00

TRANSACTIONS FOR JUNE 23-30, 2001

June 30

Cash receipts for moorage fees received by Wild Goose Marina, Inc., during the past 15 days total $6,350. These receipts have been properly credited to customer accounts in the moorage log but have not yet been entered in the Unearned Moorage Fees account in the General Journal. Total moorage fees earned during the quarter will be accounted for in the adjusting entry process. At the invoice prompt enter **MF062**.

∧∧∧

June 30

Purchased on account, and took delivery of, a new 70-foot Lake Cruiser from Snow Goose Houseboats (invoice **S5311**). This boat is the ultimate in houseboat cruisers and lists at $200,000 less a special 10% trade discount for this new model. This boat is a special order that will be delivered in the water to the customer on July 5.

∧∧

June 30

Issued a debit memo (**DM002**) and returned to Yee and Associates accessory items purchased at a total cost of $1,125. These items were purchased on account June 20 (purchase invoice **T3555**).

When all of the transactions for the final week have been entered, run the trial balance to the screen and check your account totals against the figures in the **"Check It Out"** block. If your totals do not match the check figures, carefully check the journal entries, locate the error/s, and enter the necessary correction/s. **Remember that the most efficient way to locate errors is to print a copy of the General Journal and the Trial Balance!**

101	Cash	$ 156,718.42
103	Short-Term Investments	119,999.50
105	Accounts Receivable	82,372.83
109	Notes Receivable	225,500.00
131	Service & Shop Supplies	2,773.52
145	Service & Shop Equipment	231,365.00
165	Leasehold Improvements	400,000.00
201	Accounts Payable	199,613.47
203	Short-Term Notes Payable	270,000.00
204	Discount on Short-Term Notes Payable	3,025.00
215	Unearned Moorage Fees	91,230.00
223	FICA Taxes Payable	8,275.58
227	Federal Unemployment Taxes Payable	185.07
235	Long-Term Lease Liability	6,000.00
236	Discount on Lease Financing	871.12
241	Long-Term Notes Payable	105,000.00
303	Contributed Cap. in Excess of Par, Pref. Stock	10,000.00
304	Contributed Capital--Retirement of Pref. Stock	1,250.00
307	Common Stock Dividend Distributable	0.00
420	Sales Commissions Earned	20,200.00
501	Purchases--Houseboats	1,497,400.00
502	Purchases Discounts--Houseboats	23,390.00
503	Transportation-In--Houseboats	38,230.00
506	Purchases Ret., & Allow.--Accessories & Parts	1,225.00
610	Delivery Expense	106.12
611	Tools Expense	220.54
621	Payroll Tax Expense	4,507.23
711	Interest Earned	7,445.19
813	Interest Expense	16,377.46
831	Loss on Short-Term Investments	2,529.00
	TRIAL BALANCE	$5,449,922.82

If all of your totals match the check figures, proceed to the **Adjusting Entries For The Quarter** section. If your totals do not match the check figures, print a Trial Balance and a General Journal. Carefully check the journal entries, locate the error/s, and enter the necessary correction/s. When **all** of your totals match the check figures, proceed to the Adjusting Entries.

WILD GOOSE MARINA, INC.

ADJUSTING AND CLOSING ENTRIES

For the Quarter Ended
June 30, 2001

ADJUSTING ENTRIES FOR THE QUARTER

Using a copy of the June 30 Trial Balance and the information and financial data shown below, record the adjusting entries for Wild Goose Marina, Incorporated. Be sure to select the **ADJUSTING** entries option. Adjusting entries **must not** be entered using the regular **DAILY** entries procedure. Corrections to adjusting entries must also be entered using the **ADJUSTING** entries option. **ALL ENTRIES MUST BE RECORDED AS OF JUNE 30, 2001, THE END OF THE SECOND QUARTER!**

A. The ending office supplies inventory is **$845.50**.

B. A total of **$1,333.75** in service and shop supplies have been used this quarter.

C. Prepare the insurance adjustment from the following policy information.

Policy One: Dated Aug. 1, 2000, 3-year policy, cost $9,000

Policy Two: Dated Jan 1, 2001, 12-month policy, cost $4,800

Policy Three: Dated April 1, 2001, 6-month policy, cost $5,840

Policy Four: Dated June 19, 2001, 6-month policy, cost $1,215
No insurance expense will be recorded for Policy Four this quarter.

D. A total of **$550** worth of advertising copy, paid for and **correctly charged** to the Advertising Expense account, will be received next quarter.

E. Accrued property taxes for the quarter total **$745**.

F. Depreciation for Service and Shop Equipment totals **$5,625** for the quarter. The service and shop equipment acquired June 26 has not been in service long enough to be depreciated this quarter.

G. Depreciation on the Trucks is charged at a rate of $.45 per mile. The trucks have been driven a total of 3,252 miles this quarter.

H. The special trailer, built by Wild Goose Marina, Inc., at a cost of $65,000, is estimated to have a salvage/residual value of $5,000 and a useful life of 10 years. Straight-line depreciation is used for this asset.

I. Depreciation of the office equipment is **$925** for the quarter.

J. Accrue the interest on the **short-term** notes receivable. Calculate the interest on each note to the nearest cent. **Use the 360-day banker's year for all interest computations.**

  Note One: $150,000, 12.5%, 90-day note dated May 18

  Note Two: $6,500, 12.5%, 60-day note dated June 5.

  Note Three: $70,000, 12%, installment note with the last principal and interest payment being received and recorded on June 5. Monthly payments are $10,000 plus interest on the unpaid balance. The date of the note is April 3, two installment payments have been made, and interest must be accrued for 27 days.

  Note Four: $19,000, 13%, 90-day note dated June 24

K. Moorage Fees Earned for the quarter total **$52,150.**

L. Additional income taxes expense for the period total **$1,065.**

M. The original cost for the Leasehold totaled $337,500 and is being amortized over fifteen years. Amortize the **quarterly** portion of the Leasehold account. Eight years remain on the lease agreement.

N. Leasehold improvements costing $406,250 were added to the facilities and are being amortized on a straight-line basis over ten years. Currently eight years remain on the lease agreement. Amortize the **quarterly** portion of the Leasehold Improvements account. The $75,000 of leasehold improvements made late in June **must not be included** as a part of this calculation.

O. By aging the accounts receivable it has been determined that the adjusted balance of the Allowance for Doubtful Accounts account should be $2,750.

P. Rent was prepaid for 6 months on April 1 of this year.

Q. Amortize the **quarterly** portion of the patent cost. The original cost of the patent totaled $3,975 and is amortized over a period of five years.

R. The unamortized portion of the organization costs totals $6,000 and is to be amortized over the next four years (16 quarters).

S. Accrue the interest on the $160,000, 12%, short-term note payable dated June 28.

T. On June 28, $110,000 was borrowed on a **short-term**, 11%, **discounted** note payable. The unadjusted carrying value of the note on June 30 is $106,975. Accrue the interest on this discounted note.

U. Equipment was purchased with a long-term, $25,000 note on June 6. Properly charge to Interest Expense (*interest method*) the portion of the Discount on Notes Payable that is the interest cost for the 24 days of June. The interest rate used in the original entry is 14%. *Refer as needed to the information in the June 6 transaction.*

V. New bonds were issued by Wild Goose Marina, Inc., on June 15th (check the transaction and journal entry for specific details.) Using the *interest method*, the discount amount amortized will total $112.20 and the interest expense will total $1,278.87. Enter the appropriate adjusting entry.

ADJUSTMENTS FOR INVENTORIES Wild Goose Marina, Inc., uses the "**adjusting entry approach**" for merchandise inventories. The beginning inventory balances are cleared by being adjusted to the **Income Summary** account (**account number 901**). The periodic ending inventory balances are then entered into the system.

W. The beginning inventory for Houseboats totals **$315,200**. The beginning inventory for Accessories and Parts totals **$41,132**. A single compound entry is the most efficient method of adjusting these account balances to $0.00.

X. The ending inventory for Houseboats totals **$785,330**. The ending inventory for Accessories and Parts totals **$34,200**.

When all of the adjusting entries have been correctly entered, **PRINT THE ADJUSTED TRIAL BALANCE!**

The check figure for the adjusted trial balance is $5,929,855.73.

The check figure for the Interest Expense account is $17,987.72.

If your totals match the check figures, you are ready to print the final financial documents. If you must check for an error, print a copy of the general journal and carefully check your adjusting entries.

When your adjusted trial balance totals match the check figures, you are ready to complete the final evaluation of the Wild Goose Marina, Inc., operations. **To obtain the necessary information to complete the final evaluation questions, PRINT ALL of the documents listed in instructions 1-5.**

1. **The financial statements for Wild Goose Marina, Inc.**

   THE CORRECT NET INCOME FOR WILD GOOSE MARINA, INCORPORATED, IS BETWEEN $124,400.00 AND $124,500.00.

2. **Schedule of Accounts Receivable**

3. **The Accounts Receivable Subsidiary Ledger**

4. **Schedule of Accounts Payable**

5. **The Accounts Payable Subsidiary Ledger**

Record the closing entries for Wild Goose Marina, Inc. This procedure in the Wild Goose Marina accounting system is an automatic function. Click on the general ledger tab. Then click on the **Closing** entries button and answer yes.

Click on the General Ledger tab and print the Post-Closing Trial Balance. Click on the ledger account icon and print the following General Ledger accounts:

101	**Cash**
105	**Accounts Receivable**
117	**Merchandise Inventory--Houseboats**
140	**Investment in Baldwin Manufacturing**
201	**Accounts Payable**
315	**Retained Earnings**
330	**Treasury Stock**
401	**Houseboat Sales**
901	**Income Summary**

Exit the Wild Goose Marina, Incorporated, accounting program. Using all of your printed documents, carefully answer the Final Evaluation questions. The questions and several of the end-of-the-quarter documents may be collected by your instructor.

Error Correction After Closing the Books

If, after closing the books, you discover an error or wish to print a corrected copy of any of the financial statements, you must go to the **General Journal** and click on the **Restore** button. Answer **Yes** and then **OK** to restore the journal and ledgers to pre-closing balances. Daily or adjusting entries can then be corrected using the **Daily Entries** or **Adjusting Entries** option and then **new copies of all corrected documents MUST be printed.** Again, close the books, print a corrected **Post-Closing Trial Balance,** and any corrected general ledger accounts. Then exit the program.

FINAL EVALUATION

WILD GOOSE MARINA, INCORPORATED

June 30, 2001

FINAL EVALUATION

WHITE GOOSE MARINA INCORPORATED

June 30, 2001

NAME_____

WILD GOOSE MARINA, INCORPORATED

SECTION_____DATE_____

1. How much cash was paid out on June 19? $_____

2-3. Check number **01043** was issued to the Department of Motor Vehicles. On what date was this check issued and what was the number of the invoice paid in full?

Date_____

Invoice Number_____

4. What is the reason for the June 28 debit entry to the Cash account? _____

5. Over the next three years the balance of the Discount on Lease Financing account will be periodically amortized to what account? _____

6. What is the Income From Operations for the quarter? $_____

Remember that for all percentage questions your answers must be rounded to two decimal positions (4.57689% = 4.58%).

Total Net Revenues for the quarter ended June 30, 2001, total $1,435,833.50.

7. Service Fees, Moorage Fees, and Sales Commissions Earned are what percent of the total *net revenues*? _____%

8. Office & Shop Salaries and Wages Expense is what percent of total Operating Expenses? _____%

9. Office & Shop Salaries & Wages Expense combined with Executive & Salespersons Salaries are what percent of the total *net revenues*? _____%

10. Advertising Expense is what percent of total Operating Expenses? _____%

11. After income taxes, which Other Expense account has the largest balance? _____

12. If more efficient operation of the business had allowed management to reduce operating expenses 2%, what would have been the Income from Operations for the quarter? $_____

13. If office and shop salaries and wages had been reduced 10% and all other **non-salary operating expenses** reduced 1%, how much would the Income from Operations have increased? $_____

14-18. *CALCULATE the Cost of Good Sold for the Houseboats and Accessories & Parts on the form provided.*

Wild Goose Marina, Incorporated
Cost of Goods Sold
For Quarter Ended June 30, 2001

Houseboats:

Beginning Houeboat Inventory, April 1, 2001		$
Purchases of Houseboats	$	
Purchases Discounts, Houseboats	_____	
Net Purchases, Houseboats	$ _____ (14)	
Transportation-In, Houseboats	_____	
Cost of Purchases, Houseboats		_____ (15)
Cost of Houseboats Available for Sale		$
Ending Houseboats Inventory, June 30, 2001		_____
Cost of Goods Sold, Houseboats		$ _____ (16)

Accessorries and Parts:

Beginning Accessories and Parts Inventory, April 1, 2001		$
Purchases of Accessories and Parts	$	
Purchases Ret. & Allowance of Accessories and Parts		
Purchases Discounts, Accessories and Parts	_____	
Net Purchases, Accessories and Parts	$ _____ (17)	
Transportation-In, Accessories and Parts	_____	
Cost of Purchases, Accessories and Parts		_____
Cost of Accessories and Parts Available for Sale		$
Ending Accessories and Parts Inventory, June 30, 2001		_____
Cost of Goods Sold, Accessories and Parts		$ _____ (18)

* *

19. The combined transportation-in costs for houseboats and accessories & parts total? $_____

20. If 25% of the discounts on houseboat purchases had not been taken this quarter, how much of an increase would there have been in the cost of goods sold--houseboats? $_____

21. The Gross Profit for houseboats is what percent of houseboat sales?   _____%

22. Gross Profit for houseboats was 17.02% in 2000. Is the margin for 2001 a favorable change?   YES____NO____

23. The Gross Profit for accessories & parts is what percent of total net accessories & parts sales?   _____%

24. Income from Operations is what percent of total *net revenues*?   _____%

25. In 2000 the Income from operations was 8.45% of *net revenues*. Is the total for 2001 a favorable change?   YES____NO____

26. Cost of Goods Sold--Houseboats is what percent of Houseboat Sales?   _____%

27. Executive & Salespersons Salaries are what percent of total Operating Expenses?   _____%

28. Total Operating Expenses for 2000 were 17.77% of total *net revenues*? Is the percentage for 2001 a favorable change from 2000?   YES____NO____

29. What percentage of net income can be attributed to the gain on short-term investments?   _____%

30. What percentage of net income can be attributed to Earnings On Investments?   _____%

31. What is the value of net Accounts Receivable? $_____

32. What is the book value of the Service & Shop Equipment? $_____

33. What is the total accumulated depreciation to date on the Trailers? $_____

34. How much has the Investment In Baldwin Manufacturing changed this month (June)? $_____

35. What is the current ratio?   _____

36. What is the acid-test (quick) ratio? Include Cash, Short-Term Investments, Accounts Receivable, Notes Receivable and Interest Receivable in your calculation.   _____

37. Does Wild Goose Marina, Inc., have enough cash on hand to meet current liabilities?

   YES_____ NO_____

38. What is the June 30 working capital?

   $_____

39. What is the total debt to total equity ratio (percentage)?

   _____%

40. What is the return on common stockholder's equity (ending) for the quarter? Use Net Income and assume the quarterly preferred cash dividend totals $2,500.

   _____%

41. Using average inventory, calculate the inventory turnover for the quarter.

   _____

42. Calculate the times fixed interest charges are earned. (Use income before interest and taxes)

   _____

43. What is the carrying value of the Long-Term Lease Liability?

   $_____

44. What is the carrying value of Long-Term Notes Payable?

   $_____

45. If Wild Goose Marina, Inc., has 23,230 shares of stock outstanding, what is the earnings per share (on Net Income) for the quarter? The preferred cash dividend for the quarter totals $2,500.

   $_____

46. Assuming that Preferred Stock is non-cumulative and non-participating, What is the equity per share for common stock?

   $_____

47. What is the total contributed capital from common stock?

   $_____

48. What amount of retained earnings is unrestricted (unappropriated) on June 30?

   $_____

49. After closing, what is the balance of the Income Summary account?

   $_____

50. If, at the end of the quarter, the Retained Earnings account had a deficit balance of $50,000, what would be the total stockholders' equity of the company?

   $_____

51. Is the lease payment on June 30 for a capital (financing) lease or an operating lease?

   _____

52. How much investment is "tied up" in the leasehold and leasehold improvements?

   $_____

53-55. Identify by name the three customers who have past-due accounts. Remember that Wild Goose Marina, Inc., extends 30-day credit to all customers.

   Customer_____

   Customer_____

   Customer_____

56. How much cash will be paid to Yee & Associates on or before July 30? $_____

57. Assuming all past-due accounts will be paid by charge customers in the first five days of July, how much cash from accounts receivable should be collected during the first 15 days of July? $_____

58. Assuming no additional charges, how much cash will be needed for accounts payable obligations the first 15 days of July? $_____

59. If the Corr Marine Supply account had not been paid on time, how much would this error have increased the cost of goods sold? $_____

60. On June 28, Wild Goose Marina issued a $110,000 note payable at a discount. What is the **effective rate of interest** on this note.   _____%

61. If the June 28 note ($110,000) had been a **loan** at 8% interest that required four equal annual payments that <u>included interest</u>, what would be the amount of a single payment? (Table B) $_____

62. If the note on June 28 ($110,000) had been a **loan** at 8% interest that required four equal annual payments <u>plus interest</u> on the unpaid balance, what would be the amount of the second payment? $_____

63-64. What was the dollar increase and the percentage increase in total merchandise Inventory from May 31 to June 30? $_____

_____%

65. On June 30, Wild Goose Marina, Inc., received a $6,000 dividend check from Baldwin Manufacturing. The investment in Baldwin Manufacturing is accounted for under the "equity method." If the investment was accounted for under the "cost method", what account would be credited for the $6,000?   _____

Wild Goose Marina, Inc.

OPTIONAL PROBLEMS

OPTIONAL PROBLEM A

Statement of Cash Flows

List in chronological order the **investing** activities that would be reported on a **Statement of Cash Flows**, for the month of June only. Show uses of cash from **investing** activities with brackets. *Notes Receivable from customers are considered to be operating activities (note of June 6).*

	Date	Investing Activities	Provided or Used
1.	____	_____	$_____
2.	____	_____	_____
3.	____	_____	_____
4.	____	_____	_____
5.	____	_____	_____
6.	____	_____	_____
7.	____	_____	_____
8.	____	_____	_____
9.	____	_____	_____
10.	____	_____	_____

Total Cash Provided or (Used) by Investing Activities $=============

List in chronological order the **financing** activities that would be reported on a **Statement of Cash Flows**, for the month of June only. Show uses of cash from **financing** activities with brackets.

	Date	Financing Activities	Provided or Used
1.	____	_____	$_____
2.	____	_____	_____
3.	____	_____	_____
4.	____	_____	_____
5.	____	_____	_____

OPTIONAL PROBLEM A (continued)

6. ____ _____ $_____

7. ____ _____ _____

8. ____ _____ _____

9. ____ _____ _____

10. ____ _____ _____

11. ____ _____ _____

12. ____ _____ _____

13. ____ _____ _____

Total Cash Provided or (Used) by Financing Activities $=============

14. By examining the beginning and ending Cash account balance
and the findings above for the cash provided or used by
investing and **financing** activities, determine the amount of $_____
cash used by **operating** activities during the month of June.

15-16. What was the single, largest amount of cash used by operating $_____
activities and on what date did it occur?

           Date_____

17. If the **investing** activities of June 22, and June 26 had
not occurred, what would have been the net cash provided or
(used) by **investing** activities during the month of June? $_____

18. What financing activity provided the single largest amount of cash?

_____

19. If the **financing** activity that provided the largest amount of
Cash had not occurred, what would have been the amount of the
ending balance in the cash account on June 30? (Indicate a $_____
credit balance with brackets.)

20. What investing activity used the single largest amount of cash?

_____

OPTIONAL PROBLEM B

Bond Sinking Fund Schedule

On June 15, 2001, Wild Goose Marina, Inc., issued $400,000 in Series Two, 7%, 5-year Bonds. Assume that an annual bond sinking fund deposit is required at the end of each year with the first deposit being made June 15, 2002. Using Table C in the appendix, complete the sinking fund bond schedule shown below.

Wild Goose Marina, Incorporated
Sinking Fund Schedule
Series Two Bonds

Issue Date	June 15, 2001	
Bond Par Value	$ 400,000.00	
Periods of Fund Deposits	5	
Sinking Fund Interest Rate	5.50%	

Annual Deposits Required $ 71,680.00

End of Year	Amount Deposited	Interest Earned on Fund Balance	Balance in Fund After Deposit and Interest
June 15, 2002	_____	_____	_____
June 15, 2003	_____	_____	_____
June 15, 2004	_____	_____	_____
June 15, 2006	_____	_____	_____

1. How much interest will be earned on sinking fund investments from June 15, 2002, until June 15, 2003, assuming the fund will earn the estimated 5.5 percent interest? $_____

2. How much interest will be earned on sinking fund investments from June 15, 2003, until June 15, 2004, assuming the fund will earn 5.5 percent interest? $_____

3. If the sinking fund final balance is greater than $400,000, what account will be debited for the excess?   _____

4. Over the five-year period, how much cash will actually be deposited by Wild Goose Marina, Inc., into the account? $_____

OPTIONAL PROBLEM C

Depreciation Schedule
Service and Shop Equipment--Forklift

On June 26, 2001, Wild Goose Marina, Inc., acquired, on a trade, a new forklift for use in the business service operations. Assuming that the depreciation will be recorded on **a quarterly basis**, complete the forklift depreciation schedule for the next five quarters shown below. For the units-of-production method, round the cost-per-unit to the nearest cent before computing the quarterly depreciation. Use the completed schedule to answer the questions presented.

Wild Goose Marina, Incorporated
Depreciation Schedule
Service and Shop Equipment—Fork Lift

Acquired: June 26, 2001
Asset Cost: $ 39,520.00
Salvage Value: $ 4,520.00
Life in Years: 5
Estimated Life in Hours: 30,700

Quarter	Year	Straight-Line	Declining Balance	Units-of-Production	Hours of Use
3rd	2001	_____	_____	_____	1420
4th	2001	_____	_____	_____	1600
1st	2002	_____	_____	_____	1520
2nd	2002	_____	_____	_____	1800
3rd	2002	_____	_____	_____	1750

1. Assuming straight-line depreciation is used, what will be the book value of the forklift at the end of 2001? $_____

2. If declining balance depreciation is used, what will be the book value of the forklift on June 30, 2002? $_____

3. If units of production depreciation is used, will be the total depreciation expense recorded on the forklift for 2001? $_____

4. If units-of-production depreciation is used for the forklift, what will be the book value of the asset on March 31, 2002? $_____

Wild Goose Marina, Incorporated

APPENDIX

APPENDIX
Wild Goose Marina, Incorporated

TABLE A

Present Value of $1 at Compound Interest

Time Period	7.00%	8.00%	10.00%	12.00%	14.00%	16.00%
1	0.9346	0.9259	0.9091	0.8929	0.8772	0.8621
2	0.8734	0.8573	0.8264	0.7972	0.7695	0.7432
3	0.8163	0.7938	0.7513	0.7118	0.6750	0.6407
4	0.7629	0.7350	0.6830	0.6355	0.5921	0.5523
5	0.7130	0.6806	0.6209	0.5674	0.5194	0.4761
6	0.6663	0.6302	0.5645	0.5066	0.4556	0.4104
7	0.6227	0.5835	0.5132	0.4523	0.3996	0.3538
8	0.5820	0.5403	0.4665	0.4039	0.3506	0.3050
9	0.5439	0.5002	0.4241	0.3606	0.3075	0.2630
10	0.5083	0.4632	0.3855	0.3220	0.2697	0.2267

APPENDIX
Wild Goose Marina, Incorporated

TABLE B

Present Value of $1 at Compound Interest

Time Period	1.75%	2.00%	3.50%	4.00%	7.00%	8.00%
1	0.9828	0.9804	0.9662	0.9615	0.9346	0.9259
2	0.9659	0.9612	0.9335	0.9246	0.8734	0.8573
3	0.9493	0.9423	0.9019	0.8890	0.8163	0.7938
4	0.9330	0.9238	0.8714	0.8548	0.7629	0.7350
5	0.9169	0.9057	0.8420	0.8219	0.7130	0.6806
6	0.9011	0.8880	0.8135	0.7903	0.6663	0.6302
7	0.8856	0.8706	0.7860	0.7599	0.6227	0.5835
8	0.8704	0.8535	0.7594	0.7307	0.5820	0.5403
9	0.8554	0.8368	0.7337	0.7026	0.5439	0.5002
10	0.8407	0.8203	0.7089	0.6756	0.5083	0.4632
11	0.8263	0.8043	0.6849	0.6496	0.4751	0.4289
12	0.8121	0.7885	0.6618	0.6246	0.4440	0.3971
13	0.7981	0.7730	0.6394	0.6006	0.4150	0.3677
14	0.7844	0.7579	0.6178	0.5775	0.3878	0.3405
15	0.7709	0.7430	0.5969	0.5553	0.3624	0.3152
16	0.7576	0.7284	0.5767	0.5339	0.3387	0.2919
17	0.7446	0.7142	0.5572	0.5134	0.3166	0.2703
18	0.7318	0.7002	0.5384	0.4936	0.2959	0.2502
19	0.7192	0.6864	0.5202	0.4746	0.2765	0.2317
20	0.7068	0.6730	0.5026	0.4564	0.2584	0.2145

Present Value of $1 Received Periodically For A Number Of Periods

Time Period	1.75%	2.00%	3.50%	4.00%	7.00%	8.00%
1	0.9828	0.9804	0.9662	0.9615	0.9346	0.9259
2	1.9487	1.9416	1.8997	1.8861	1.8080	1.7833
3	2.8980	2.8839	2.8016	2.7751	2.6243	2.5771
4	3.8309	3.8077	3.6731	3.6299	3.3872	3.3121
5	4.7479	4.7135	4.5151	4.4518	4.1002	3.9927
6	5.6490	5.6014	5.3286	5.2421	4.7665	4.6229
7	6.5346	6.4720	6.1145	6.0021	5.3893	5.2064
8	7.4051	7.3255	6.8740	6.7327	5.9713	5.7466
9	8.2605	8.1622	7.6077	7.4353	6.5152	6.2469
10	9.1012	8.9826	8.3166	8.1109	7.0236	6.7101
11	9.9275	9.7868	9.0016	8.7605	7.4987	7.1390
12	10.7395	10.5753	9.6633	9.3851	7.9427	7.5361
13	11.5376	11.3484	10.3027	9.9856	8.3577	7.9038
14	12.3220	12.1062	10.9205	10.5631	8.7455	8.2442
15	13.0929	12.8493	11.5174	11.1184	9.1079	8.5595
16	13.8505	13.5777	12.0941	11.6523	9.4466	8.8514
17	14.5951	14.2919	12.6513	12.1657	9.7632	9.1216
18	15.3269	14.9920	13.1897	12.6593	10.0591	9.3719
19	16.0461	15.6785	13.7098	13.1339	10.3356	9.6036
20	16.7529	16.3514	14.2124	13.5903	10.5940	9.8181

APPENDIX
Wild Goose Marina, Incorporated

TABLE C

Factors for Determining Deposits to Sinking Fund

Time Period	2.75%	3.00%	5.50%	6.00%	11.00%	12.00%
1	1.0000	1.0000	1.0000	1.0000	1.0000	1.0000
2	0.4932	0.4926	0.4866	0.4854	0.4739	0.4717
3	0.3243	0.3235	0.3157	0.3141	0.2992	0.2963
4	0.2399	0.2390	0.2303	0.2286	0.2123	0.2092
5	0.1893	0.1884	0.1792	0.1774	0.1606	0.1574
6	0.1556	0.1546	0.1452	0.1434	0.1264	0.1232
7	0.1315	0.1305	0.1210	0.1191	0.1022	0.0991
8	0.1135	0.1125	0.1029	0.1010	0.0843	0.0813
9	0.0994	0.0984	0.0888	0.0870	0.0706	0.0677
10	0.0882	0.0872	0.0777	0.0759	0.0598	0.0570
11	0.0791	0.0781	0.0686	0.0668	0.0511	0.0484
12	0.0715	0.0705	0.0610	0.0593	0.0440	0.0414
13	0.0650	0.0640	0.0547	0.0530	0.0382	0.0357
14	0.0595	0.0585	0.0493	0.0476	0.0332	0.0309
15	0.0548	0.0538	0.0446	0.0430	0.0291	0.0268
16	0.0506	0.0496	0.0406	0.0390	0.0255	0.0234
17	0.0469	0.0460	0.0370	0.0354	0.0225	0.0205
18	0.0437	0.0427	0.0339	0.0324	0.0198	0.0179
19	0.0408	0.0398	0.0312	0.0296	0.0176	0.0158
20	0.0382	0.0372	0.0287	0.0272	0.0156	0.0139

APPENDIX
Wild Goose Marina, Incorporated

Wild Goose Marina, Inc.
Trial Balance
May 31, 2001

	Debit	Credit
Cash	$ 221,015.23	
Petty Cash	100.00	
Short-Term Investments	142,017.00	
Accounts Receivable	131,121.75	
Allowance for Doubtful Accounts		$ 2,517.00
Notes Receivable	355,550.00	
Subscriptions Rec., Common Stock	122,250.00	
Merch. Inventory--Houseboats	315,200.00	
Merch. Inventory--Access. & Parts	41,132.00	
Prepaid Insurance	19,640.00	
Prepaid Rent	24,000.00	
Office Supplies	1,243.00	
Service & Shop Supplies	1,952.00	
Invest. in Baldwin Manufacturing	207,559.70	
Long-Term Investments	1,250,000.00	
Service & Shop Equipment	188,520.00	
Accum. Deprec., Ser. & Shop Equip.		40,355.00
Trucks	48,550.00	
Accumulated Deprec., Trucks		28,250.00
Trailers	65,000.00	
Accumulated Deprec., Trailers		6,000.00
Office Equipment	12,960.00	
Accumulated Deprec., Office Equip.		4,220.00
Leasehold	180,000.00	
Leasehold Improvements	325,000.00	
Patents	3,180.00	
Organization Costs	6,000.00	
Accounts Payable		278,300.00
Interest Payable		2,000.00
Short-Term Notes Payable		90,000.00
Preferred Cash Dividends Payable		4,000.00
Common Cash Dividends Payable		21,600.00
Salaries & Wages Payable		39,355.23
Sales Tax Payable		17,842.70
Unearned Moorage Fees		72,550.00
Employee's Fed. Income Taxes Pay.		7,355.00
FICA Taxes Payable		8,007.50
State Unemployment Taxes Payable		278.14
Federal Unemployment Taxes Payable		92.71
Long-Term Lease Liability		6,500.00
Discount on Lease Financing	1,008.41	

Continued next page...

Continue from previous page...

Trial Balance

	Debit	Credit
Long-Term Notes Payable		90,000.00
Bonds Payable		200,000.00
Premium on Bonds Payable		4,567.36
Preferred Stock		200,000.00
Cont. Cap. in Ex. of Par, Pref. Stock		20,000.00
Common Stock		2,000,000.00
Common Stock Subscribed		200,000.00
Cont. Cap. in Ex. of Par, Cm. Stk.		50,000.00
Retained Earnings		119,422.36
Cash Dividends Declared	26,000.00	
Houseboat Sales		904,500.00
Accessories & Parts Sales		37,333.00
Access. & Parts Sales Ret. & Allow.	370.00	
Service Fees Earned		38,115.00
Sales Commissions Earned		15,100.00
Purchases--Houseboats	676,000.00	
Purchases Discounts--Houseboats		9,400.00
Transportation-In--Houseboats	13,105.00	
Purchases--Accessories & Parts	13,862.60	
Purch. Ret. & Allow.--Acc. & Parts		100.00
Purch. Disc.--Accessories & Parts		497.45
Trans.-In--Accessories & Parts	320.00	
Office & Shop Salaries & Wages Exp.	73,200.00	
Executive & Salespersons Salaries	36,000.00	
Equipment Rental Expense	3,000.00	
Truck Operating Expense	2,450.00	
Advertising Expense	2,250.00	
Credit Card Expense	295.21	
Delivery Expense	62.12	
Tools Expense	86.50	
Deprec. Expense, Office Equipment	400.00	

Continued next page...

Continue from previous page...

Trial Balance

	Debit	Credit
Electric & Gas Expense	1,312.00	
Telephone Expense	904.00	
Bank Service Charges	73.00	
Cash Short and Over	8.00	
License Expense	712.00	
Professional Services Expense	615.00	
Janitorial Services Expense	612.00	
Miscellaneous Expense	74.12	
Interest Earned		4,201.19
Dividends Earned		2,311.00
Gain on Sale of Assets		1,250.00
Gain on Short-Term Investments		200.00
Miscellaneous Revenue		56.00
Interest Expense	10,125.00	
Loss on Sale/Disposal of Assets	50.00	
Loss on Short-Term Investments	135.00	
Loss on Long-Term Investments	1,256.00	
Total	$4,526,276.64	$4,526,276.64

```
Wild Goose Marina, Inc.
Schedule of Accounts Receivable
Last Activity Date: May 31, 2001
```

Number	Name	Balance
10200	Adams Farms Incorporated	19,000.00
10550	Bettencourt, Inc.	57,000.00
10820	R. J. Corsetti	2,150.00
11050	J. P. Elam	.00
11185	Joan Kuhlman	.00
11260	Kingston & Sons, Inc.	.00
11350	Dale Novice	550.00
11405	Randy Robberts	1,000.00
11470	Roseburg & Associates	.00
11520	Taylor Company	2,670.00
11695	Tisedaile Const. Co.	42,251.75
11920	Zakk, Incorporated	6,500.00
Total		$131,121.75

```
Wild Goose Marina, Inc.
Schedule of Accounts Payable
Last Activity Date: May 31, 2001
```

Number	Name	Balance
20500	Corr Marine Supply	12,650.00
21990	Foster Business Supply	5,650.00
22600	Kruzer Houseboats	260,000.00
24800	Luzzi, Incorporated	.00
25950	Quinlivin, Incorporated	.00
26675	Reading Real Estate	.00
27005	Rockwood Business Supply	.00
27125	Snow Goose Houseboats	.00
28400	Yee & Associates, Inc.	.00
Total		$278,300.00